The NAFTA

*What's In,
What's Out,
What's Next*

*Richard G. Lipsey
Daniel Schwanen
Ronald J. Wonnacott*

Policy Study 21
C.D. Howe Institute

C.D. Howe Institute publications are available from:
Renouf Publishing Company Limited, 1294 Algoma Road,
Ottawa, Ontario K1B 3W8; phone (613) 741-4333; fax (613) 741-5439

and from Renouf's stores at:
71½ Sparks Street, Ottawa (613) 238-8985
211 Yonge Street, Toronto (416) 363-3171

For trade book orders, please contact:
McGraw-Hill Ryerson Limited, 300 Water Street,
Whitby, Ontario L1N 9B6; phone (416) 430-5050

Institute publications are also available in microform from:
Micromedia Limited, 165 Hôtel de Ville, Place du Portage, Phase II,
Hull, Quebec J8X 3X2

This book is printed on recycled, acid-free paper.

Canadian Cataloguing in Publication Data

Lipsey, Richard G., 1928–
    The NAFTA : what's in, what's out, what's next

(Policy study, ISSN 0832-7912 ; 21)
Includes bibliographical references.
ISBN 0-88806-334-2

1. Canada – Treaties, etc. 1992 Oct. 7.
2. Free trade – North America. 3. North America –
Commercial treaties. 4. Canada – Commercial policy.
I. Schwanen, Daniel. II. Wonnacott, Ronald J., 1930–   .
III. C.D. Howe Institute. IV. Title. V. Series: Policy study
(C.D. Howe Institute) ; 21.

HF1766.L5 1994   382′.917   C94-931379-3

Cover design by Leroux Design Inc.
Printed in Canada by Kromar Printing Ltd.,
Winnipeg, Manitoba, July 1994.

Contents

Foreword

These are times of continuing rapid change in the world trading environment, as global trade patterns are being reshaped by technological progress and investment flows. At the same time, protectionist threats continue to grow, as national leaders remain under constant pressure from noncompetitive forces in their respective political arenas.

While we can rejoice at the successful completion of the most recent round of trade negotiations under the GATT, it is clear that the evolution of up-to-date and detailed multilateral trading rules tends to lag, sometimes severely, the challenges posed by protectionist threats. Thus, for close trading partners, regional trade agreements can help to bridge the gap until the multilateral process catches up.

It was in this context that, on January 1, 1994, Canada, Mexico, and the United States implemented the North American Free Trade Agreement (NAFTA). The effects of this lengthy and complex document on the climate in which Canadian firms conduct international business will be felt for decades, as they and the governments under which they operate adapt to its provisions. Other countries are likely to seek to join the newly constituted free trade area, and the NAFTA's innovations will influence the future direction of multilateral trade negotiations.

Many Canadians, however, are unfamiliar with the NAFTA's provisions. Others remain fearful of Canada's place in a comprehensive trade agreement with one country, the United States, that is so much bigger, and another, Mexico, that is clearly poorer but hoping to close that gap by attracting investments from other parts of the world. Canadians remain unconvinced, despite the fact that smaller economic partners in trade agreements tend to benefit from them by virtue of being less subject to the protectionist vagaries of the larger international market.

This study, by three of Canada's leading trade policy experts, is meant to help nonexperts familiarize themselves with the content of the deal, and also to point out what is *not* in it. In so doing, the study debunks some of the myths, both economic and political, surrounding the NAFTA. The authors root the agreement in past Canadian trade policy, describe the provisions of the agreement under five broad headings, and assess its likely impact on the economy and on Canada's sovereignty.

The authors conclude that many of the concerns expressed about the NAFTA are not grounded in the letter of the agreement itself or in previous experience with trade agreements. On the contrary, they say, with all its imperfections, the NAFTA is a useful set of rules that allows smaller trading nations, such as Canada and Mexico, to expand their markets in the face of global protectionist tendencies.

This being said, the NAFTA is not a panacea for all the trade problems Canada is experiencing with the United States or other partners in the hemisphere. Too often, access to markets remains painfully restricted, but many of the deal's provisions are a useful base from which to secure further opening.

The C.D. Howe Institute's aim in presenting studies such as this is to raise the level of public debate on issues of national interest by presenting diverse points of view — whether or not it agrees with them — in publications that are well researched and well grounded. The Institute hopes that, in so doing, it will give Canadians much to think about, including the information they require to exercise their responsibilities as citizens.

This volume was copy edited by Darlene Zeleny and desktop published by Brenda Palmer. The analysis and opinions presented in the study are the responsibility of the authors and do not necessarily reflect the view of the Institute's members or Board of Directors.

Thomas E. Kierans
President and
Chief Executive Officer

Acknowledgments

We wish to acknowledge the contributions of the presenters and discussants at a symposium on the NAFTA held at the C.D. Howe Institute in December 1992, and to thank them for their insights into what was then a new, and complex, document. This book draws in many ways on the papers presented at the conference by Rick Barichello, Armand de Mestral, Lorraine Eden, Michael Gestrin, Brenda González-Hermosillo, Jon Johnson, Tim Josling, Maureen Molot, André Plourde, Alan Rugman, Pierre Sauvé, Murray Smith, and William G. Watson. Most of these papers were published in 1993 as "The NAFTA Papers" in the *C.D. Howe Institute Commentary* series.

We also wish to thank David Brown and Bill Robson at the C.D Howe Institute, Michael Hart at External Affairs Canada, and Gordon Ritchie of Strategico Inc. for their reviews of early versions of this book. We are particularly grateful to Jonathan Fried, Sandy Moroz, and Bruce Stockfish at External Affairs Canada for conducting a very helpful review of the factual material presented in parts of the study. On the production side, the volume's copy editor, Darlene Zeleny, and Barry Norris, the C.D. Howe Institute's Director of Publications, patiently handled numerous revisions to the book. It goes almost without saying that all the remaining errors and omissions are the authors' responsibility.

Richard G. Lipsey,
Daniel Schwanen,
Ronald J. Wonnacott

Introduction

The North American Free Trade Agreement (NAFTA) is a historic agreement among Canada, the United States, and Mexico to liberalize their trade. The pact was agreed to in principle in August 1992 and signed in December 1992. Parallel accords on environmental and labor standards were reached in August 1993, and the NAFTA took effect on January 1, 1994.

This book surveys the policy context in which the NAFTA is being implemented, and assesses its impact on Canada's economy and policymaking. The study's unique feature is its core section: a guide, for nonspecialists, to the agreement itself. It includes a description of the NAFTA's provisions in summary form, and a view of their significance in the context of the General Agreement on Tariffs and Trade (GATT), the bilateral Canada-US Free Trade Agreement (FTA), and Canada's trade policy objectives.

Part 1 of the book, consisting of Chapters 1–3, is the Overview. In Chapter 1, we summarize the economic structure and performance of the three NAFTA countries, and paint a picture of recent global trade and investment trends. Chapter 2 puts the NAFTA in the context of Canada's trade policy agenda. Chapter 3 is an outline of the agreement itself, particularly in relation to the existing Canada-US FTA.

The detailed description of the NAFTA provided in Part 2 (Chapters 4–8) covers provisions affecting trade in goods (Chapter 4); services, investment, and related issues (Chapter 5); government procurement (Chapter 6); environmental and labor standards (Chapter 7); and dispute settlement (Chapter 8). Each chapter is divided into four sections: what the NAFTA says; how it differs from the FTA and the GATT; the significance of its provisions; and the concerns, if any, that we or other analysts have about the provisions.

Readers who are not interested in the detailed description of the NAFTA that constitutes Part 2 can skip to Part 3, which surveys the

NAFTA's impact on Canada. Chapter 9 assesses whether Canada achieved its negotiating objectives with the NAFTA, and Chapter 10 surveys what we know about the likely economic impact of the deal. To complete Part 3, Chapter 11 addresses the issue of whether the agreement imposes unacceptable constraints on the policies of Canadian governments, a frequent criticism of this and other trade deals.

In broad terms, we conclude that the NAFTA will have a positive impact on Canada. Our assessment is that Canada's participation in the agreement is consistent with the need to improve its position in a changing global economy, but that the agreement does not constitute a radical departure from traditional Canadian trade policy. The NAFTA is expected to have a small positive impact on the Canadian economy as long as Canada remains party to the agreement. Nonparticipation would have meant losses for Canadians, and locating investment in Canada would have become less attractive relative to locating in the United States.

The NAFTA opens up new avenues for Canadian exporters. Most will benefit from clearer rules of access to the US market and better dispute avoidance mechanisms than those that were in place under the FTA. Businesses in specific sectors — notably services, energy, and all sectors affected by restrictive government procurement policies — will gain better access to the United States and Mexico. The FTA's dispute settlement mechanism, which has proved beneficial to Canadian exporters, has been incorporated into the NAFTA, with some modifications, on a permanent basis.

Because of certain tradeoffs contained in the NAFTA, however, not all of its provisions represent gains for Canada. In particular, the NAFTA may make it more difficult in the long run for non-North American car producers and for clothing manufacturers located in Canada to penetrate the US market. Moreover, modifications to the dispute settlement regime that seem small on the surface may in some, but probably not many, cases make it less likely that the dispute settlement panels will decide in favor of Canadian exporters.

While Canada may not have achieved all its negotiating objectives, neither did Mexico or the United States, the two economies that will be most affected by the NAFTA. Overall, the NAFTA preserves the principle of "national treatment," whereby each country remains free to adopt and enforce the standards and measures it considers necessary to achieve economic, social, and environmental well-being. In the light of this fact, one can reject the view that the deal will compel Canada to harmonize its economic and social policies with those of its neighbors to the south.

It is also clear, however, that the NAFTA is by no means a panacea for Canada's trade problems. This is mainly because producers in each country remain vulnerable to the possibility that the other countries will impose antidumping and countervailing duties. The recently concluded Uruguay Round of the GATT, while enhancing the positive effects of the NAFTA in a number of areas, will provide only useful first steps toward a significant improvement in this area. Consequently, much work remains to be done to provide Canadian-based producers with even more secure access to the US and other major markets. In this respect, it is important that Canada actively pursue negotiations with the United States on a bilateral subsidies and dumping code, which the Canadian government made a precondition for implementing the NAFTA. The small chance that these negotiations will result in substantial complementary agreements that will enhance the benefits of the NAFTA and its precursor agreement, the Canada-US FTA, must be exploited.

Part I

Overview

Chapter 1

The Global Context

Current Global Trends in Trade and Investment

Trade

The freeing of international trade has been one of the engines of postwar economic expansion, particularly since the first successful negotiations toward a General Agreement on Tariffs and Trade (GATT) in 1947. The industrialized countries today export and import substantially more as a proportion of their output than they did 40 years ago. In fact, during the past four decades this rising trend has continued essentially uninterrupted, and has recently been spurred by rapid growth in services trade, in addition to merchandise trade.

Building on their access to major markets in Europe and North America, many countries that would have been considered as developing only 30 years ago have now joined the ranks of the industrialized. Chief among them are Japan and the "newly industrialized" countries (NICs) of Southeast Asia. If not for the remaining barriers to trade throughout the world — for example, in textiles and agricultural products — many more countries could have enjoyed rapid development.

However, the industrialized countries in general, and the United States in particular, have made it more difficult for the NICs and other would-be exporters to their markets to emulate Japan's strategy of export-led growth. Since the 1980s, they have increasingly made accepting imports conditional on rules pertaining to government subsidies, openness in financial markets, respect for intellectual property, and transparent regulations in the domestic market of the exporting country — rules with which Japan, in an earlier period, did not have to contend. The industrialized countries also enhanced their trade remedy arsenal during the 1980s, notably with the growth of managed trade measures that are not covered by the GATT (such as so-called voluntary export restraints) and with their declared intention of unilaterally enforcing a "level playing field" on countries that penetrate their markets.

Analysts may disagree on how the threatened rise in unilateralism might affect global trade, but it is certain to make the "Japan Inc." model, as it applied to external trade relations, a thing of the past. Judging by the demands for greater openness that the United States and Europe placed on countries such as South Korea and Taiwan during the 1980s (not to mention the pressures they put on Japan itself),[1] it is unlikely that any other country will be able to follow Japan's example in the future. The negotiations toward a North American Free Trade Agreement (NAFTA) clearly took place within this context of increased debate over the impact of policies affecting trade, both directly and indirectly.

Investment and the Transnational Corporation

Although international trade in goods and services continued to grow through the 1980s, the most important development in cross-border exchanges during that decade was the growth of international investment flows. While all such investment flows have implications for the conduct of economic policy, foreign direct investment (FDI) — as opposed to portfolio investments or short-term capital flows — is of particular importance in terms of future trade flows and the conduct of trade policy.

---

1 These pressures by the United States on Japan were renewed in early 1994, following the conclusion of the Uruguay Round of the GATT. The United States complains that Japan maintains informal barriers to trade, such as the rules that govern its retail sector. See "US Launches New Japan Assault," *Financial Post*, January 26, 1994, p. 11.

FDI can come in the form of either the greenfield establishment of a new business in a given country by nonresidents or the acquisition by foreign interests of a controlling equity share in a domestic enterprise. Although many less-developed countries with low labor costs have increasingly liberalized their rules on foreign direct investment, most FDI flows during the 1980s were, in fact, toward North America and Europe. There are many reasons for this, including the type of investments being made (acquisitions of existing businesses have dwarfed greenfield investments) and the fact that successful investment in new ventures requires a lot more than low labor costs.

Indeed, a main reason for FDI in Europe and North America is that these are the richest markets overall. Proximity to one's market is often important to winning customers in that market — not only because of low transport costs, but also because of factors such as the need to maintain close contact with customers of sophisticated products. In addition, in contrast to the less-developed countries, developed countries can offer large pools of skilled labor. They also have the supporting infrastructure — telecommunications, transportation, support services for business — that is a key requirement for competing in the global economy. Thus, the importance of wage differentials has been greatly exaggerated as a factor influencing FDI for a number of manufacturing and service industries.[2]

Competition for Foreign Investment and the Market for Unskilled Labor

The expansion of FDI has in turn spurred new growth areas in international trade, as suggested by the high level of intrafirm trade in North America and the recent flow of trade following Japanese investment in Southeast Asia. Both free trade and FDI allow produc-

2 In a recent survey of top managers at Canada's 1,000 largest companies, labor costs ranked behind availability of skilled employees, the exchange rate, quality of infrastructure, and market access in a list of factors affecting competitiveness. See "Lower Tax Rates Not Lower Wages Top NAFTA Lure Survey Shows," *Toronto Star*, May 3, 1993, p. C1.

ers in any one country to be plugged into an international network of clients, suppliers, financing, joint venture alliances, and firms linked by ownership. Within these networks, producing units compete for the right to be the network's global supplier of a particular good or service not only on the basis of cost, but also in terms of management skills, product quality, and, ultimately, customer satisfaction. An extensive survey conducted by the Conference Board of Canada concludes that,

> [a]ccording to the respondents [all of them transnational corporations], product mandates are replacing the geographic mandates that had traditionally driven their production. For example, a particular plant may have the proprietary knowledge of a product within the scope of the entire company, rather than simply taking care of the Canadian market.[3]

Location remains key, however, since enterprises are ultimately able to achieve their objectives only if the original or host location is able to provide certain elements, including access to a sizable market, a strong labor force and other resources, and favorable national and local economic and social policies. Of growing importance is the host location's openness to trade, without which the production facility has access to neither the markets nor the international inputs necessary for it to maintain its competitiveness.

Growth in international investment and sourcing has now reached the point where countries that have resisted the trend and tried to retreat behind protectionist walls will find themselves at a serious disadvantage relative to their more open competitors. But greater openness leading to worldwide sourcing can also create problems, since it allows goods whose production requires only a low level of skill increasingly to be made in low-wage countries.[4]

---

3 Stephen Krajewski, *Intrafirm Trade and the New North American Business Dynamic*, Conference Board of Canada Report 88-92 (Ottawa: Conference Board of Canada, 1992), p. 2.

4 Richard G. Lipsey, *Notes on Globalisation and Technological Change and Canadian Trade Policy*, CIAR Program in Economic Growth and Policy, Working Paper 8 (Toronto: Canadian Institute for Advanced Research, February 1993).

And with low-wage, low-skilled countries vying for investment in product areas in which the technology has become standardized, the market for less skilled labor has become more globalized. Although industrialized countries do try to resist some of the downward pressure this might impose on their unskilled wage rates, such a policy jeopardizes their chances of attracting the kind of investment that would help maintain the higher-value-added industries crucial to their long-term economic success.

Creating Comparative Advantage and Systems Friction

The difficult tradeoff between protecting unskilled wage rates and the need to open up trade and investment raises the question whether comparative advantage can be created through active government policy in the areas of training, research, and development and public infrastructure and institutions.

In many countries, such a focus on "outward-looking" domestic policies that encourage exports is replacing the former reliance on now-discredited "inward-looking" policies that restrict imports — including high tariffs, subsidies to weak sectors of the economy, and investment barriers. As a result of this shift, however, international trade relations have come to focus on a new type of friction, which Canadian trade policy expert Sylvia Ostry has called "systems friction."[5] Different systems of domestic policies used to be accepted as background noise to the international game of competition in selling goods. Today, with the increasing recognition that domestic policies may be used to shape comparative advantage, trade conflicts arise over domestic policies in areas as diverse as the environment, labor market practices, distribution systems, and government procurement. Strong pressures are exerted either to harmonize these policies or to "manage" the trade that is affected by them in order to produce

---

5 Sylvia Ostry, *Governments and Corporations in a Shrinking World* (New York: Council on Foreign Relations, 1990).

the desired result. Maintaining an open trading environment in the face of such conflicts is one of the major tasks confronting trade policymakers today, a task that is very different from the challenge that trade negotiators faced in the postwar period — that of removing barriers at the border.

Mexico: A New Free Trade Partner for Canada and the United States

GDP, Growth, and Inflation

Mexico is the world's thirteenth-largest economy. In 1991, its gross domestic product (GDP) of US$287 billion was approximately 50 percent as large as Canada's (US$593 billion), but only 5 percent as large as that of the United States (US$5.673 trillion). On a per capita basis, Mexico's GDP was approximately US$3,300 in 1991, similar to that of countries such as Greece and Portugal.[6] By comparison, in 1991, Canadians and Americans enjoyed a per capita GDP of $22,000 and $22,400, respectively.

Growth in the Mexican economy was brutally interrupted in the early 1980s. The prolonged crisis was brought about by the collapse of oil prices — oil was Mexico's single most important export — and the country's subsequent inability to service its high external debt, combined with the early dampening effects of stabilization policies undertaken by the Mexican government.[7] Indeed, whereas fixed capital investment in the Mexican economy grew at an average annual rate of 8.5 percent in real (after-inflation) terms from 1965 to 1980, the 1980s saw an average annual decline of

---

6 World Bank, *World Development Report, 1993* (Washington, DC, 1993); and International Monetary Fund, *International Financial Statistics, 1992* (Washington, DC, 1993).

7 For additional background material on Mexico, see Organisation for Economic Co-operation and Development, "Survey of Mexico" (Paris, December 1992); International Monetary Fund, "Mexico: The Strategy to Achieve Growth," Occasional Paper 99 (Washington, DC, September 1992); and *Financial Times of London Survey on Mexico* (November 1992).

5 percent. This slowdown was accompanied by an increase in infla-tion, which peaked at more than 160 percent in 1987, and a decline in real wages of about 40 percent over the course of the decade. Mexico's economic performance contrasts sharply with that of Canada and the United States, which experienced somewhat faster economic growth and lower rates of inflation in the 1980s than in the 1970s.

In the 1990s, however, the story has been different so far. Mexico's real GDP has been increasing steadily, if unspectacularly, while the Canadian and US economies experienced a recession from which they only began to emerge in 1993.

Population

In mid-1991, Mexico's population was about 88 million; Canada's was roughly 27 million; and that of the United States was about 253 million. The populations of Canada and the United States, on the one hand, and that of Mexico, on the other, differ significantly in age composition. With more than a third of its people currently under 15 years of age, Mexico's population is expected to grow to more than 140 million by 2025, an increase of 65 percent from the current level, whereas the populations of Canada and the United States are expected to increase by only about 20 percent over the same period.

Industry

Manufacturing accounts for a larger share of GDP in Mexico than in either Canada or the United States. This reflects the usual pattern of developing countries over the past 30 years — namely, that the most important shift in the composition of their output has been away from agriculture and into manufacturing, whereas the most import-ant shift over the same period in the output of developed countries has been away from manufacturing and into services. Services ac-count for a smaller share of output in the Mexican economy than they do in the Canadian or US economies (61 percent of GDP in Mexico, compared with 69 percent in the United States and 67 percent in Canada). In contrast, Mexico's primary sector (of which two-thirds is agriculture) still accounts for more than 10 percent of GDP, whereas the primary sectors of Canada and the United States hover around 5 percent.

Mexico's employment structure differs even more substantially from those of Canada and the United States. More than a quarter of Mexico's labor force is employed in the agricultural sector, which produces less than 7 percent of Mexico's output. Thus, in terms of output per worker, the agricultural sector is the least productive sector of the Mexican economy. By contrast, just over 11 percent of the labor force is employed in the manufacturing sector, which accounts for almost one-quarter of Mexico's GDP, making that sector very productive relative to other broad sectors of the economy. Although manufacturing is the sector with the highest output per worker in Canada and the United States as well, the contrast in its productivity relative to that of other sectors of the economy is not nearly as extreme as in Mexico. On average, however, the output per worker in Canadian and US plants remains far superior to that in Mexican plants.[8]

Exports and Imports

The United States is by far the most important export market for both Mexico and Canada, accounting for 68 percent of Mexican exports and 76 percent of Canadian exports in 1991. (The European Union and Japan are the second- and third-largest markets, respectively, for both Canada and Mexico.) Although Canada and Mexico are the United States' largest and fourth-largest export markets, respectively, neither receives a dominant share of total US exports. Further-

---

8 See Canada, Department of Finance, *The North American Free Trade Agreement: An Economic Assessment from a Canadian Perspective* (Ottawa: Supply and Services Canada, 1992); and Lorraine Eden and Maureen Appel Molot, "Comparative and Competitive Advantage in the North American Trade Bloc," *Canadian Business Economics* 1 (Fall 1992): 45–59.

more, exports are significantly less important as a share of domestic output for the United States than they are for Canada or Mexico.

As a result of the decline in oil prices in the early 1980s, but also because it succeeded in developing new competitive industries during that decade, Mexico saw a much larger shift in the composition of its exports during the ten-year period from 1981 to 1991 than did either Canada or the United States. The value of Mexico's petroleum and petrochemical exports fell from US$14.6 billion in 1981 — almost 70 percent of the country's exports at the time — to $8.2 billion — just over a quarter of total Mexican exports in 1991. Mexico's manufacturing exports picked up the slack over that period, growing at an astonishing 17 percent per year, from US$3.4 billion in 1981 to $16.0 billion in 1991. In particular, exports in the automotive industry enjoyed a 33 percent annual growth rate. Over the same period, Mexican exports of machinery and equipment, including electronic equipment, rose by 21 percent a year, on average. These shifts have caused Mexico's broad export structure to become more like those of Canada and the United States — particularly with respect to the importance of transportation equipment — although Mexico continues to exhibit a stronger reliance on primary commodities for its exports than do either Canada or the United States.

In contrast to its export performance, Mexico imported less each year from 1982 through 1988 than it did in 1981, reflecting the country's economic problems during that period. After three years of rapid growth (1989–91), however, attributable to a rebounding economy as well as to new trade liberalization measures, imports are now almost 60 percent above their 1982 peak.

Trade in services occupies a very important place in Mexico's external transactions, with services exports (mainly tourism) accounting for more than 30 percent of total exports of goods and services. The comparable figures for the United States and Canada are 23 percent and 11 percent, respectively. Imports of services are also important in Mexico, accounting for about a quarter of total imports, compared with 16 percent in Canada and 17 percent in the United States.

Internal and
External Policy Regimes

The shifts in economic policies that took place in both Canada and the United States during the 1980s, although significant, pale in comparison with the changes in Mexico during the same period. These policy changes pertained to the external debt problem (to which we referred earlier), the budget, inflation and exchange rates, the regulation of internal domestic activity, controls on foreign investment, and trade.

Mexico's *external debt* had become an enormous millstone around that economy's neck, finally giving rise to a moratorium on principal repayments, in August 1982. (The moratorium came to represent the formal beginning of the worldwide "debt crisis" of the less-developed countries.) It was almost impossible for Mexico to emerge from the crisis with its development prospects intact. Investors had to believe not only that Mexico's internal reforms were genuinely intended to wean the economy away from its previous dependence on oil and government borrowing, but also that new investment would be safe. The crisis was resolved only in 1989, with the announcement of the Brady Plan, an agreement on debt restructuring supported by the United States, Japan, and multilateral institutions. The agreement helped to produce a sharp reduction in the perceived risk of investing in Mexico. This, in turn, generated falling interest rates and, for the first time since the oil boom, net inflows into Mexico of both long- and short-term private capital.

With respect to *budgetary policy*, Mexico's public sector deficit averaged about 10 percent of GDP annually between 1977 and 1985, then rose to about 15 percent of GDP in 1986 and 1987, following a devastating earthquake and the collapse of oil prices. The 1989 debt agreement improved the budgetary situation by allowing Mexico to regain its creditworthiness while sharply reducing debt-servicing payments from their original levels. By 1991, Mexico's public sector was in virtual financial balance. In contrast, public sector deficits in Canada and the United States, which had remained large during the economic expansion of the 1980s, ballooned during the recession of the early 1990s to 6.3 and 3.4 percent, respectively, in 1991.

Canada and the United States performed similarly with respect to *inflation* during the ten years following the 1982 recession: inflation in the United States averaged about 4 percent over that period, and in Canada about 5 percent. (Inflation in the United States has tended to be lower than inflation in Canada at times when the US dollar has been overvalued, but now, as a result of Canada's tight monetary policy of the late 1980s, Canadian inflation is lower.) In contrast, Mexico experienced runaway inflation as it struggled to reorient its economy following the debt and oil crises, and its central bank was forced to fund the budget deficit. The removal of price and exchange-rate controls in the late 1980s also contributed to the rapid increase in prices. Great strides have been made since 1987, when inflation peaked and the Mexican government and unions signed a Pact of Economic Solidarity ("Pacto"). The pact, which is still being renewed periodically, amounts to a prices and incomes policy aimed at a return to budgetary and monetary discipline (by fixing the exchange rate between the Mexican peso and the US dollar) with minimal costs in terms of economic growth and employment. Nevertheless, at nearly 10 percent, Mexican inflation remains well above that of its two NAFTA partners — a source of concern in an economy that is once again expanding.

During the 1980s, Canada, the United States, and Mexico all attempted to improve their economies' capacity to adapt to change by lessening some of the *regulatory burden on domestic activity* and by privatizing state enterprises. Once again, the most profound changes occurred in Mexico, where the level of state control in the economy was initially higher than in either the United States or Canada and where pressures for change were great. Mexico's privatization program, which the Organisation for Economic Co-operation and Development has characterized as one of the most extensive in the world, was accompanied by deregulation, notably in the financial sector, trucking, telecommunications, and foreign trade. Unlike Canada and the United States, however, the Mexican government is

adamant that there will be no privatization of "strategic" government enterprises — in particular, Petroleos Mexicanos (PEMEX),
which exercises a monopoly on the country's oil sector and accounts
for 20 percent of the Mexican government's revenues.

Mexico, like Canada, has also been actively pursuing *foreign
direct investment*. In Canada, the Foreign Investment Review Agency
was replaced in 1985 by Investment Canada, with the objective of
promoting foreign investment. In Mexico, after the 1910 revolution
and the nationalization of foreign oil companies in 1938, the climate
toward FDI had generally been hostile; it became more relaxed with
the passage in 1965 of the law that introduced in-bond manufacturing (maquiladoras). Current guidelines have considerably stream-
lined FDI approval procedures and have opened up many sectors to
foreign investment. Nevertheless, control of a large number of key
sectors is still reserved for the state or for Mexican nationals. In the
United States, since the mid-1980s, a surge of FDI inflows and
high-profile acquisitions of domestic property by nonresidents has
spurred calls for more stringent reviewing of both foreign investment and the taxation practices of foreign transnationals. At the state
level, however, competition to attract new investment remains fierce.

In conjunction with its initiatives in the area of domestic liberalization, Mexico also liberalized its *trade policy*. Mexico joined the
GATT in 1986 and greatly accelerated the pace of trade liberalization
following the 1987 Pacto, in the hope that imports would help put
downward pressure on domestic prices. Between 1982 and 1989,
Mexico's average tariff (weighted by the value of imports to which
particular tariff rates applied) fell from 16.4 percent to 9.5 percent.
More important, nontariff barriers to trade were removed at a fast
pace: whereas in 1982 all imports were subject to licensing restrictions, only 17 percent of the value of all imports was still subject to
such restrictions in 1989. (Licensing restrictions remain only in the
agricultural, automobile, electronics and pharmaceutical sectors.)

Canada and the United States also made strides in the direction
of trade liberalization during the past decade, notably with the
Canada-US Free Trade Agreement, which came into effect in 1989.

Even before, however, the two countries had enjoyed much freer trade with each other and with the rest of the world than did Mexico.

Toward Hemispheric Free Trade

Since 1985, Mexico has also pursued a number of bilateral initiatives pertaining to trade and investment with the United States. These culminated, in 1990, in a request by the Mexican government for free trade negotiations, which led to the NAFTA. Many analysts see the NAFTA, which even critics of the Mexican government concede is popular in that country, as the crowning achievement of current government's market-oriented policies, and as a mechanism that will encourage Mexico to remain committed to its recent reforms; any future Mexican government that might seek to reverse the reforms will face greater obstacles now that they have been under-written by an international trade agreement. Moreover, the NAFTA goes beyond this to commit Mexico to further important reforms in many areas. This, in turn, enhances the chances of success of existing reforms by making the country more attractive for FDI.

Inflows of FDI, combined with a deliberately slow transition period to full free trade, are key elements of Mexico's free trade plan, designed to compensate for the dislocation caused by free trade in agriculture and other relatively inefficient sectors by stimulating rapid growth elsewhere in the economy. In an important way, a smooth pace of adjustment in Mexico would also be to the advantage of the United States: as some critics of the NAFTA have pointed out, a huge displacement of Mexican agricultural workers could have the effect of keeping manufacturing wages in Mexico from rising quickly, with the result that job losses would threaten certain vulnerable categories of US workers.[9]

---

9 See, for example, Jeff Faux and Richard Rothstein, *Fast Track, Fast Shuffle: The Economic Consequences of the Administration's Proposed Trade Agreement with Mexico* (Ottawa: Canadian Centre for Policy Alternatives, April 1991). Note that the structural adjustment funds that the European Community made available to Europe's poorer countries during the transition to a single market were meant, in part, to ease such problems.

The United States, for its part, was interested in negotiating a trade agreement with Mexico for a number of reasons. In the 1980s, many US observers became increasingly critical of the pace and content of the GATT process, and had come to see the European Community and Japan as economic rivals that used "unfair" means to penetrate the US market. Such views were influenced by a range of factors, including the emergence of an unprecedented US trade deficit, continuing state intervention in economic affairs in both Europe and the Far East, increasing economic integration in those regions, and the decline of the communist threat worldwide. The NAFTA offered the United States a chance to strengthen its own competitive position and to promote its vision of how the "systems friction" among industrialized countries, on the one hand, and between the industrialized countries and the developing countries, on the other hand, could be resolved.

At the same time, the United States was placing greater emphasis on security and prosperity in the Western Hemisphere as a geopolitical aim, as reflected in the Bush administration's Enterprise of the Americas initiative. In that regard, the NAFTA was seen as a vehicle that would strengthen recent Mexican reforms and that might eventually encourage other Latin American countries to become part of the regional free trade area. Furthermore, the United States was experiencing bilateral problems with Mexico, including illegal immigration from Mexico and what was perceived as "back door" entry into the US market through the maquiladoras. Such problems, it was argued, could be resolved through a regional agreement. For all these reasons, the United States acceded to Mexico's request to negotiate.

With a number of countries expressing interest in joining a future hemispheric agreement, Canada could not afford to be excluded from a decision by Mexico and the United States — its chief competitor and its major market — to enter into negotiations that could shape the economic future of the Americas.

Chapter 2

Canada's Trade Policy Agenda

Historical Background

Canada is a relatively small trading nation operating in a world undergoing the turbulent process of globalization. Exports provide much of its economy's lifeblood. But these exports are sold in international markets that are becoming increasingly difficult to penetrate because of the changing nature of trade barriers and fierce competition from new suppliers. Opening international markets, and keeping them open, has been a consistent theme in Canadian trade policy this century — not surprising in a country whose economic strengths have evolved from its raw materials base to include manufacturing and services. How does Canada's involvement in the Canada-US Free Trade Agreement (FTA) and the NAFTA fit into this policy?

The Years Leading Up to the GATT

The 1930s were watershed years in the trade policy of the industrialized countries. Standards of living around the world were damaged by increases in US tariffs, first with the *Tariff Act* of 1922 and then with the more than 50 percent increase under the *Smoot-Hawley Tariff Act* of 1930 and the subsequent retaliation by other countries. Recognizing this, the Roosevelt administration reversed the United States' trade policy as early as 1934, when it persuaded Congress to give it the authority to enter into trade agreements that would sharply reduce tariff levels.

Canadians experienced first-hand the devastating effects of the rise in worldwide protectionism in the early 1930s, at a time when the United States had begun to overtake Britain as Canada's major export market.[1] Canada took advantage of the US *Reciprocal Trade Agreements Act* of 1934, negotiating a treaty in 1935 that led, in 1938, to what was in effect a three-way set of framework agreements between Canada, Britain, and the United States. The 1938 agreements were narrower in scope than even the short-lived reductions of duties contained in the 1854 Reciprocity Treaty between Canada and the United States. Nonetheless, those agreements can be seen in retrospect as the precursor of the General Agreement on Tariffs and Trade (GATT), to which 23 contracting parties agreed in 1947 in the aim of liberalizing multilateral trade.[2]

The GATT to 1985

Canada participated in and benefited from the successive GATT negotiating rounds, which, in the early stages, focused on bringing new members into the agreement and cutting tariffs on merchandise trade. This approach achieved enormous reductions in tariff barriers among the signatories, and unleashed the strong growth in world trade that was vital to the postwar economic expansion.[3]

With the Kennedy Round of the mid-1960s and the Tokyo Round of the 1970s, however, the approach adopted by the GATT

---

1 Economic depression in the United States and the onset of World War II resulted in Britain's regaining its position as Canada's major export market between 1932 and 1941. The United States regained top spot in 1942.

2 See J. Harvey Perry, "The Great Trade Debate," *Tax Memo* (Canadian Tax Foundation) 71 (August 1986). The Reciprocity Treaty was abrogated by the United States in 1866. A similar treaty fell through in 1911, when Canadians chose not to re-elect the Liberal government that had negotiated it. Thus, we see that Canada had traveled the road of bilateral trade agreements early in its history.

3 These gains were achieved in large part because the results of bilateral negotiations that were at the core of the GATT rounds were extended to all GATT contracting parties by virtue of the "most favored nation" rule. See Sidney Golt, *The GATT Negotiations, 1986–90: Origins, Issues, and Prospects* (London; Washington, DC; Toronto: British-North American Committee, 1988), p. 6.

countries began to show its limitations. The reduction of tariffs to only a fraction of their prewar levels served to reveal other existing barriers to trade — and, what was worse, to encourage the adoption of new, nontariff barriers. Many of the latter were much more difficult to eliminate than barriers that were imposed at the border, because they were far less transparent, consisting of "internal" policies of states, such as subsidies, technical standards, and government procurement practices. The issue of disciplining the use of antidumping and countervailing duties[4] and managed trade measures, which are contrary to the spirit but not to the letter of the GATT, also came to the fore. Despite a new multilateral deal reached at the end of 1993, the GATT has only been partially successful in dealing with some of these increasingly important issues, although it has managed very significant progress in other areas, notably the long-sought-for integration of agriculture and textiles into the overall framework of the agreement.

Deepening the Canada-US Trade Relationship

Given the growing importance of Canada-US trade, it is not surprising that many issues of vital importance to Canada have been addressed bilaterally, resulting in sectoral trade agreements in such sectors as agricultural machinery (in the 1920s); defense products (in the 1940s); and automotive products, with the Canada-US auto pact (in the 1960s).

In the early 1970s, the Canadian government adopted a policy of attempting to diversify its economic links in order to reduce its

---

4 Antidumping duties are imposed by an importing country on imported goods that are priced at less than the "normal" price charged in the exporter's domestic market or are otherwise judged to be priced unfairly, and that are deemed to cause material injury to the importing country's industry as a result. Countervailing duties are imposed by an importing country to offset government subsidies in the exporting country when the subsidized products are deemed to cause material injury to the importing country's industry.

dependence on the United States. Despite significant efforts,[5] this "third option" was, on balance, unsuccessful. One reason was that any truly effective bilateral or multilateral accord to liberalize Canada's trade with third countries would have come at the expense of the United States, and no third country was prepared to jeopardize its trade relationship with the United States for the sake of liberalizing its relatively unimportant trade with Canada. By 1983, Ottawa had resumed its earlier policy of seeking sectoral trade arrangements with the United States.

The FTA in Canadian Trade Policy

Meanwhile, a growing number of observers were advocating taking a serious look at comprehensive free trade with the United States. Their main argument was that manufacturing productivity in Canada, and therefore Canadians' standard of living, was constrained by the short production runs and other inefficiencies associated with servicing a small market.[6] It was also pointed out that the lack of competition in the domestic market resulted in higher prices for consumers and inhibited innovation and the economy's competitiveness in the long run.

Of course, these arguments supported multilateral free trade as well. However, both defensive and offensive arguments were made in favor of bilateral free trade with the United States as the most realistic policy option.[7] Arguments on the defensive side were based on evidence that US protectionism was once again on the rise. Acting

---

5 See Gordon Mace and Gérard Hervouet, "Canada's Third Option: A Complete Failure?" *Canadian Public Policy* 15 (December 1989): 387–404.

6 See, for example, Arthur J.R. Smith, "Canada's Policy Problems," in H.E. English, ed., *Canada and the New International Economy* (Toronto: University of Toronto Press, 1961), especially pp. 59–63; and Ronald Wonnacott and Paul Wonnacott, *Free Trade between the United States and Canada: The Potential Effects* (Cambridge, Mass.: Harvard University Press, 1967).

7 See, in particular, Richard G. Lipsey and Murray G. Smith, *Taking the Initiative: Canada's Trade Options in a Turbulent World*, Observation 27 (Toronto: C.D. Howe Institute, 1985).

bilaterally to eliminate all tariffs and contain the use of nontariff barriers was seen as a more effective way of dealing with the problem than waiting for the results of a new GATT round that would involve roughly a hundred other countries. Whereas opponents argued that Canada would be the loser in any bilateral trade negotiations with the much larger United States, supporters pointed out that small countries have more to gain from imposing a rules-based system than do large countries, which can expect to be the winners in an unregulated trading environment.

Arguments on the offensive side maintained that the increased complexity of regional trade issues required a more solid framework than the GATT could offer. Other countries, particularly in Europe, provided a model of liberalizing regional trade without rejecting the multilateral framework. Many Canadians believed that their economy had matured to the point that it could compete head-to-head with other economies throughout world. Since the 1930s, Canadian industries had successfully weathered the removal of 80 percent of their tariff protection, and it was time to remove the last 20 percent in order to allow secure benefits that would the more successful Canadian industries to compete in the global marketplace.

Economists have always understood that free trade would mean severe adjustments for some Canadian industries,[8] and many prescribed adjustment assistance for those industries. Such was the recommendation of the Royal Commission on the Economic Union and Development Prospects for Canada (Macdonald Commission) in its report issued in the fall of 1985. Overall, however, the Macdonald Commission concluded that a bilateral trade agreement with the United States was especially worth exploring.[9] Shortly after the

---

8 See, for example, Richard Harris and David Cox, *Trade, Industrial Policy, and Canadian Manufacturing*, Ontario Economic Council Research Study 31 (Toronto: Ontario Economic Council, 1983); and Economic Council of Canada, *Venturing Forth: An Assessment of the Canada-US Trade Agreement* (Ottawa: Supply and Services Canada, 1988).

9 Canada, Royal Commission on the Economic Union and Development Prospects for Canada [Macdonald Commission], *Report*, vol. 1 (Ottawa: Supply and Services Canada, 1985), pp. 323–445.

publication of the commission's report, the Canadian government decided to open bilateral free trade negotiations with the United States. Those negotiations resulted in the 1987 Canada-US FTA, which was implemented on January 1, 1989. There was, however, no special adjustment program to help workers or industries affected by the agreement.

Canada's Decision to Join the NAFTA

As in the case of the FTA, reasons based on both defensive and offensive perspectives supported Canada's decision, in early 1991, to join the free trade talks that were planned between Mexico and the United States. To understand those reasons, it is useful to consider what would have happened had Mexico and the United States signed a bilateral agreement to which Canada was *not* a party.[10]

The situation that would have resulted if Canada and Mexico had each had a free trade agreement with the United States would best be described by the "hub-and-spoke" model of trade arrangements. In this model, one country, "the hub," has preferential market access to two or more trading partners, the "spokes," through a series of bilateral arrangements. Such a situation would have had five major consequences for Canada in terms of access to its trading partners' markets:

1.   Once Mexico and the United States had signed a free trade agreement, Canadian firms in the US market would have faced increased competition from Mexican-based producers, since Mexico would have shared Canada's preferential access to the US

---

10 The following is drawn from Richard G. Lipsey, *Canada at the US-Mexico Free Trade Dance: Wallflower or Partner?* C.D. Howe Institute Commentary 20 (Toronto: C.D. Howe Institute, August 1990); Ronald J. Wonnacott, *US Hub-and-Spoke Bilaterals and the Multilateral Trading System,* C.D. Howe Institute Commentary 21 (Toronto: C.D. Howe Institute, October 1990); and idem, *The Economics of Overlapping Free Trade Areas and the Mexican Challenge* (Toronto; Washington, DC: Canadian-American Committee, 1991).

market. The same consequence would result from a trilateral agreement, such as the NAFTA, but Canada, by joining that agreement, can at least ensure that Mexican producers will not enjoy *more favorable conditions in the US market than do Canadians*. (As an example, in the NAFTA, the United States provided more open access to government procurement contracts than it had conceded to Canada in the bilateral FTA.)

2.   If Canada had been left as a spoke by not taking part in the NAFTA, Canadian exporters would have been at a disadvantage relative to US exporters in the Mexican market: US firms would have had preferential tariff-free access to Mexico, while Canadian exporters would not.

3.   If Canada had not been a party to the NAFTA, US producers alone would have had access to duty-free Mexican inputs and would thus have gained a competitive advantage over their Canadian counterparts.

4.   Perhaps an even more important consequence of two separate US bilateral agreements with Canada would have been their effect on *investment*: The United States would have been the only location from which a producer would have had free trade access to all three markets, an arrangement that would have diminished Canada's attraction for FDI. (Of course, the severity of this problem would have depended on the nature of the rules of origin and the degree of security of access to the large market provided in the free trade agreement: the more liberal the rules, the greater the loss to Canada for remaining outside the agreement.)

5.   If Canada had wished to enter the NAFTA at a later date, it would probably have had to accept the conditions already set by the NAFTA partners at that time.

The preceding list comprises the major "defensive" reasons behind Canada's decision to join the negotiations. But Canada's participation in the NAFTA was not simply a case of "reluctant regionalism."[11] The NAFTA negotiations also afforded Canada an opportunity to address sticking points that resulted from, or had been neglected under, the FTA, such as disputes over natural gas exports and the role of Asian "transplants" in automobile manufacturing. Furthermore, because the NAFTA could eventually become a hemispheric agreement with full Canadian participation, it would have a similar effect to that of a multilateral GATT agreement in diffusing US influence on Canada's trade.

The NAFTA and Canada's Multilateral Objectives

The proliferation of regional trade agreements has raised some concerns. Although they are permitted under the rules of GATT Article XXIV, regional agreements derogate from the original GATT principle of extending to *all* parties the trade-liberalizing measures agreed to by any two or more of them. Known as the most-favored-nation principle, this rule has constituted one of the fundamental levers of postwar trade liberalization.

The attraction of regional agreements, however, is that they allow the participating countries to bring to the table issues of specific relevance to them, and to tackle those issues directly with their more important trading partners. The alternative is to wait years for a global agreement, which, in any event, is almost certain to address specific regions' major concerns only partially. Moreover, innovations negotiated at the regional level can constitute the basis of subsequent GATT negotiations.

Canada's involvement in the NAFTA offers a case in point: the country's recent focus on trade within North America has certainly not diminished its commitment to the cause of multilateral trade

---

11 A term used by Al Berry, Leonard Waverman, and Ann Weston in "Canada and the Enterprise for the Americas Initiative: A Case of Reluctant Regionalism," *Business Economics* 15 (April 1992).

liberalization. Indeed, Canada was a firmly committed participant in the recently completed Uruguay Round of GATT negotiations.

There appears to be no *a priori* reason why the FTA or the NAFTA should be deemed inconsistent with Canada's multilateral commitments and objectives. Trade issues today are not what they were in the immediate postwar period, and special instruments to resolve them have had to be considered in conjunction with the GATT. Regional trade agreements are one such instrument.

In the light of current realities, then, it is not surprising that many of the issues discussed in the NAFTA negotiations — including intellectual property rights, investment, trade in services, subsidies, government procurement, and, of particular importance for Canada, supply management programs for certain agricultural products — were also on the table at the Uruguay Round of the GATT. And it was certainly not a surprise that the results of the latter did not lead the Canadian economy down a fundamentally different path than the one taken with the FTA or the NAFTA.

Chapter 3

The NAFTA in Outline

The Nature of Free Trade Areas

The North American Free Trade Agreement creates a free trade area that encompasses Canada, Mexico, and the United States. In a nutshell, the agreement

- eliminates all tariffs on trade in goods among the three countries on a schedule that will be virtually completed in ten years, with the bulk of the tariffs to be substantially reduced or eliminated in the earlier years;
- greatly liberalizes trade in services as well as access to government procurement contracts among the three signatories;
- provides substantial protection for investors against discriminatory practices in partner countries, as well as ensuring protection for intellectual property;
- recognizes the right of each country to adopt any health, safety, environmental, or other standards it requires on its territory, even if this means denying entry to goods, services, or investments from another NAFTA country;
- builds on the experience of the Canada-US Free Trade Agreement (FTA) to improve many aspects of that agreement, including clarifying rules of origin that caused disputes under the FTA (the record here is, however, mixed: in some sectors, the NAFTA's new rules of origin will actually be somewhat more restrictive of trade); and

• establishes a set of institutions for resolving trade and investment-related disputes that, despite some significant differences, is based largely on the FTA model.

The NAFTA establishes a free trade area rather than some other, more embracing, type of trade-liberalizing arrangement, such as a customs union or an economic union. The distinctive feature of a free trade area is that member countries remain free to pursue their own trade policies *vis-à-vis* nonmembers. In contrast, a customs union requires that members adopt a set of common commercial policies toward nonmembers. The much more inclusive economic union requires in addition that members harmonize many of their domestic economic and social policies.

Of course, any trade agreement — whether bilateral or multilateral — requires that the participating countries liberalize trade with one another. Although a free trade agreement leaves member governments free to adopt almost any policies pertaining to their own residents (individuals and firms) that they wish, those policies may not discriminate between goods or services produced by their own residents and goods or services produced by others within the free trade area, unless this is explicitly allowed by the agreement. In other words, each country is free to pursue different policy objectives on virtually any matter, as long as the policies do not amount to disguised ways of discriminating against residents of other member countries in sectors liberalized by the agreement. The application of this "national treatment" principle — which is also found in the General Agreement on Tariffs and Trade (GATT) — underlies much of the NAFTA, as it did the FTA.

Because a free trade area allows each member to have different tariffs and other restrictions on trade with nonmembers, it requires the establishment of

• *rules of origin*, to identify goods that are substantially produced within the free trade area and are thereby entitled to move duty free across borders between member countries — that is, across the area's internal borders; and

- *customs points along internal borders*, to ensure that only goods substantially made within the free trade area — that is, goods that meet the rules of origin — are granted the right of free movement.

If rules of origin and customs checks were not required, non-member countries would simply export goods to the member country posting the lowest external tariff and then have the goods trans-shipped duty free to the other member countries. The effect of such "trade deflection" would be to force all member countries to lower their tariffs toward nonmember countries to the lowest tariff levied by any member country. (Such problems do not arise in a customs union because members share a unified policy toward nonmembers, and a good entering the area is consequently subject to the same tariff regardless of which country it enters. Thus, as long as it is truly liberalizing its internal trade, a customs union requires neither scrutiny at internal borders nor rules of origin.)

Rules of origin are typically one of the most controversial areas of any free trade negotiation, since they will determine in practice whether a good is allowed to move duty free between partner countries or whether it must continue to pay the applicable tariff in the importing member country.

The NAFTA's Rules of Origin in Broad Outline

As was the case under the FTA, there are three possible ways in which a good can qualify as originating in North America, and thus move duty free between member countries of the NAFTA:

- It may be "wholly obtained or produced" in one of the NAFTA countries. This would be the case, for example, for many raw materials and/or agricultural goods, or for any manufactured good produced *entirely* from such goods. For example, a maple table produced in Canada and using nails made from minerals extracted in the territory of Canada, the United States, or Mexico would be treated as "originating" — that is, qualifying under the rules of origin — because it would contain no foreign material.

- The good may contain material that originates outside the NAFTA, as long as that material has been substantially transformed in a NAFTA country, as prescribed by the agreement — for example, if imported steel is transformed into a refrigerator in one of the NAFTA countries.

- In addition to the requirement in the previous point, or in some cases as an alternative rule, some products are considered "originating" only if they meet a regional value content requirement, whereby a certain percentage of their contents must originate within the NAFTA countries.

There are two methods for calculating regional value content — the net cost method and the transaction value method. Most goods — except apparel, textiles, automobiles, and certain agricultural products, to which special rules of origin apply — will satisfy the content requirement if at least 50 percent of their net cost or 60 percent of their transaction value originates in North America. In most cases, a producer is free to choose the method of calculation.[1]

The NAFTA and the FTA Compared

The NAFTA came into force on January 1, 1994 — that is, only five years after the bilateral FTA between Canada and the United States took effect. Because many Canadians are still assessing the impact of the first agreement and because, on many issues, the NAFTA negotiators were responding to the perceived advantages and defects of the NAFTA, we offer a summary table comparing the two agreements in Table 1.

---

1 See Jon R. Johnson, *What Is a North American Good? The NAFTA Rules of Origin,* C.D. Howe Institute Commentary 40 (Toronto: C.D. Howe Institute, February 1993).

Table 1:   *An Overview of How the NAFTA Relates to the FTA*

Topic	NAFTA Reference	FTA Reference	Comments on Key Differences between the NAFTA and the FTA
Objectives/ definitions	Chaps. 1, 2	Chaps. 1, 2	Certain agreements on the environment supersede the NAFTA
Market access	Chap. 3	Chaps. 4, 5	Extends Canada's duty drawbacks to 1996: establishes a customs union in computers and parts
Wine and distilled spirits	Annex 312.2	Chap. 8	Extends the FTA provision to Mexico
Automobiles	Annex 300-A	Chap. 10	Gradually removes Mexican trade barriers and investment incentives
Rules of origin	Chap. 4	Chap. 3	More stringent for textiles, apparel and autos; otherwise, easier to follow and less subject to arbitrary decisions
Customs procedures	Chap. 5	Annex 406	Advance rulings on rules of origin now available
Energy	Chap. 6	Chap. 9	Allows Mexico exclusive public ownership
Agriculture	Chap. 7	Chap. 7	Separate Canadian and US regimes toward Mexico.
Safeguards	Chap. 8	Chap. 11	Ensures fair and open proceedings.
Standards	Chap. 9	Chap. 6	Provides added openness with regard to development of and conformity to standards
Government procurement	Chap. 10	Chap. 13	Expands coverage to services and construction

Table 1:   *An Overview of How the NAFTA Relates to the FTA* - cont'd.

Topic	NAFTA Reference	FTA Reference	Comments on Key Differences between the NAFTA and the FTA
Investment	Chap. 11	Chap. 16	Expands coverage to more types of properties; introduces binding investor-state arbitration
Services	Chap. 12	Chap. 14	Covers all servicesnot explicitly excluded
Telecommunications	Chap. 13	Annex to Chap. 14	Improves access for providers of value-added services
Financial services	Chap. 14	Chap. 17	Gives financial services access to dispute settlement; gradually opens up Mexico
Monopolies and state enterprises	Chap. 15	Articles 2010 and 1602	Specifies rights and obligations of state enterprises
Temporary entry for business persons	Chap. 16	Chap. 15	Builds on the FTA provision; extends it to Mexico
Intellectual property	Chap. 17	Articles 2004 and 2006	The FTA dealt only with retransmission rights; NAFTA protects patents, etc.
Notification and administration	Chap. 18	Article 2102	Establishes contact points and fair proceedings with respect to changes in laws and regulations
Dispute settlement in antidumping and countervailing duty cases	Chap. 19	Chap. 19	Makes FTA system permanent, somewhat less room for favorable panel decisions
Institutions and general dispute	Chap. 20	Chap. 18	Enhances panel system

Similarly, in the following sections of the chapter, the discussion is structured as a comparison of the NAFTA and the FTA. The key features of the NAFTA are grouped into four categories: (1) important NAFTA features that remain essentially unchanged from the FTA; (2) NAFTA provisions that build on FTA provisions; (3) new areas covered by the NAFTA; and (4) NAFTA features that represent considerable departures — some positive, some negative from Canada's perspective — from the FTA.

Important Features of the FTA Remaining in Force under the NAFTA

Some of the FTA's key features governing Canada-US trade were reproduced in the NAFTA substantially unchanged. In some cases, they were extended to Mexico with certain modifications, whereas in others — in particular, in the areas of energy and agriculture — a different treatment was negotiated for Mexico. The relevant features are as follows:

National treatment. This principle refers to the nondiscriminatory treatment by NAFTA countries of one another's nationals. It is embedded in the NAFTA, as it was in the FTA. National treatment provisions pertain specifically to standards (Article 904, paragraph 5), cross-border investments (Article 1102), and services (Articles 1202 and 1405), among other areas. Their inclusion reaffirms the general principle that each country can establish its own policies in any of these areas as long as they do not discriminate against nationals of other NAFTA countries.

Tariff removal. The implementation schedule established by the FTA, wherein tariffs were to be eliminated by January 1, 1998, will continue to apply between Canada and the United States. The NAFTA provides separate tariff reduction schedules for trade between Mexico and each of the other two countries. These schedules call for the elimination of tariffs on most items within ten years, and on some particularly sensitive items within 15 years.

Energy. All provisions of the FTA pertaining to energy continue to apply between Canada and the United States under the NAFTA. The controversial proportionality provision of the FTA has also been rewritten into the NAFTA. It states that, should Canada decide to impose supply restrictions under any of the specific circumstances set out in the GATT, it may not reduce exports, as a proportion of output, below the share prevailing during the 36 months prior to the imposition of the restrictions, unless each reduction occurs in the course of normal transactions between buyers and sellers. The Canadian government issued a unilateral declaration in December 1993 stating, among other things, that it "interprets the NAFTA as not requiring any Canadian to export a given level or proportion of any energy resource to another NAFTA country." The declaration appears to have been carefully crafted to express the high priority Ottawa accords energy security, without actually contradicting the language of the NAFTA, which essentially forbids discrimination against US purchasers.

Agriculture. In agriculture, as in energy, the NAFTA retains most of the FTA provisions between Canada and the United States: virtually all of the agricultural provisions in Chapter 7 of the FTA continue to apply under the NAFTA. The NAFTA includes separate agreements between Mexico and each of the other two countries. It is worth noting that, as in the FTA, the NAFTA's section on agricultural trade between Canada and Mexico allows for the continuation of Canada's supply-management programs, through import quotas, in accordance with the terms of Article XI of the GATT, as defined in 1992. This section will likely have to be revised in view of the Uruguay Round agreement, under which equivalent tariffs will replace import quotas as a means of protecting supply-management systems for dairy and poultry — and these tariffs will be reduced over time.

Temporary entry for business persons. The provisions of this innovative chapter of the FTA remain essentially unchanged and will be extended to Mexico (with special but temporary limits on the entry of Mexican business persons to the United States).

Investment review. The right of countries to screen large incoming investment, secured under the FTA, is now entrenched in the NAFTA. The threshold above which review is allowed will remain at $150 million in Canada, whereas in Mexico, it will rise from $25 million to $150 million by the tenth year of the agreement.

Monopolies. Like the FTA, the NAFTA explicitly recognizes the right of its signatories to designate private or public sector monopolies. These monopolies must, however, treat enterprises of other NAFTA countries exactly as they do domestic enterprises with respect to the purchase or sale of the monopolized goods or services, and they must not use their position to engage in anticompetitive practices in some other, nonmonopolized market, in which an enterprise of another NAFTA country operates.

Trade remedy laws. As with the FTA, each country retains its anti-dumping and countervailing duty laws under the NAFTA. This means that Canadian producers remain exposed to the full force of US trade remedy laws, although, as with the FTA, this continuing threat is tempered by a dispute settlement mechanism capable of overturning decisions based on an unfair application of trade legislation.

Cultural industries. Cultural industries, such as book publishing and the film industry, remain exempt under the NAFTA.

Strengthening FTA Provisions in the NAFTA

The NAFTA builds on certain key provisions of the FTA, notably in the following areas:

Duty drawbacks.[2] The planned elimination of Canada's duty drawback regime under the FTA with respect to trade with the United States has been pushed back two years, to January 1, 1996.

---

2   A duty drawback is a refund of duties paid or a waiving of duties owed by an importer on a good that is subsequently re-exported, or that is used as a material in the production of another good that is subsequently exported.

Customs procedures. The NAFTA reduces uncertainty for exporters and importers by making possible advance rulings by national customs authorities on whether or not a product satisfies the rules of origin.

Government procurement. Government procurement provisions have been expanded to cover services (for contracts valued at more than US$50,000) and construction (for contracts valued at more than US$6.5 million). The threshold above which these provisions apply remains at US$25,000 for goods traded between Canada and the United States (as in the FTA), but is set at $50,000 for trade between Mexico and each of its two partners. The thresholds are higher for procurement by government enterprises (in Canada, Crown corporations) than by government departments. More Canadian and US federal entities are covered by the NAFTA than were covered by the FTA. More stringent bid tendering procedures have been included in the NAFTA — a feature that is important for Canadian suppliers in their dealings with a new free trade partner — and the FTA bid-challenge system is preserved. Another important feature of the NAFTA is that it formally opens up discussions on liberalizing procurement by state and provincial governments and government entities.

Investment. The NAFTA covers "passive investments" (for example, stocks, bonds, and real estate). The definition of the term *investor* has been broadened to include firms established in a NAFTA country (as opposed to firms owned only by nationals of a NAFTA country). Arguably the most important innovation here, however, is the introduction of a binding international arbitration mechanism to deal with disputes between investors and states. Investors who feel that a NAFTA country has not respected the provisions of the NAFTA's investment chapter can use this mechanism to claim restitution.

State enterprises. The NAFTA's national treatment principle explicitly recognizes the right of parties to establish or maintain state (or, in

Canada's case, provincial) enterprises, provided they do not discriminate in the course of business against enterprises of other NAFTA countries.

Services. With respect to telecommunication, financial, and transportation services, the NAFTA expands on the liberalization measures found in the FTA. In addition, rather than specifying a list of included services, as the FTA did, the NAFTA liberalizes more broadly by providing for free trade in services generally, except those sectors and measures the agreement specifically excludes.

Dispute settlement. The NAFTA makes permanent, and extends to Mexico, the FTA provisions that allowed for an impartial panel review of administrative decisions to impose antidumping and countervailing duties. (The FTA did not explicitly provide for those provisions to continue beyond 1995.) Certain modifications in the NAFTA provisions are, however, expected to make it more difficult for panels to contradict the determination of the US and Canadian agencies that administer trade remedies. It is not yet clear how important this change will be in practice.

New Areas Covered by the NAFTA

The environment. The three NAFTA countries have committed not to lower environmental standards to attract investment; the agreement also states that each country can adopt tough environmental standards without contravening the agreement.

Intellectual property. The chapter that addresses the protection of patents and many other types of intellectual property is new, and essentially reproduces the new GATT text on the subject.

Land transportation services. The provisions on land transportation will allow NAFTA-based operators the freedom to pick up merchandise in any NAFTA country for delivery anywhere in another country within the free trade area.

Computers. Over time, the NAFTA will create a common external tariff among the three countries on many computer products. This means that trade in computer goods within the NAFTA will be unencumbered by the need to determine origin.

Departures from the FTA

Automobiles. Although the NAFTA achieves the important objective of removing, over time, the web of trade restrictions that has protected the Mexican auto sector, its rules of origin make auto trade between Canada and the United States more restrictive in some respects than under the FTA. The tougher requirements will disadvantage the plants of non-North American producers located in Canada, but are expected to benefit North American parts producers, at least in the short run.

Apparel. New rules of origin will make it more difficult for Canadian apparel and textile producers using non-North American fabric and yarn to expand their exports to the United States beyond the quotas provided. Canadian producers are, however, compensated to some extent by an expansion of those quotas, as well as by the extension of duty drawback.

Negotiations on reforming antidumping and countervailing duties. Unlike the FTA, the NAFTA establishes no institutional mechanism and no time frame for negotiating a replacement regime for antidumping and countervailing duties. Although it was not clear what could have been expected from the mechanisms set up under the FTA (specifically, under Article 1907), their removal has left Canada farther away from its objective of eventually gaining completely secure access to the US market. In December 1993, however, the three countries agreed to conduct separate negotiations on an antidumping and subsidies code. The negotiations are scheduled to conclude in December 1995. Although this effectively reimposes the FTA time frame, the FTA's explicit goal of establishing a replacement regime has not been formally adopted as a negotiating objective.

Conclusion

Although the NAFTA builds on the FTA in many respects, it also detracts from the FTA in a few areas. It will entail significant changes, not only because it embraces Mexico, but also because it modifies elements of Canada's trading relationship with the United States. Although many of the trade-enhancing changes can easily be traced to existing provisions in the FTA, others — such as the provisions on the environment and on investor-state dispute arbitration — enter uncharted territory by the standards of international trade agreements.

These and other NAFTA provisions will be examined in more detail in the next five chapters. The final part of the book comprises three chapters that summarize the implications of the NAFTA.

Part II

The NAFTA in Detail

Chapter 4

Trade in Goods

What Does the NAFTA Say?

The rules covering trade in goods among the NAFTA countries are described in Chapters 3–9 of the NAFTA text. Three of those chapters explain the conditions under which goods from one NAFTA country will have access to another: Chapter 3, on national treatment and market access for goods; Chapter 4, on rules of origin; and Chapter 5, on customs procedures. Two chapters, as well as two annexes to Chapter 3, are devoted to special rules for specific types of goods: Chapter 6, on energy; Chapter 7, on agriculture; Annex 300-A, on trade and investment in the automotive sector; and Annex 300-B, on textile and apparel goods. Chapter 8 describes the emergency conditions under which a NAFTA country can temporarily suspend or even rescind the tariff reductions specified in the agreement. Finally, Chapter 9 deals with technical barriers to trade in the form of standards. Because these measures are applicable primarily to trade in goods, Chapter 9 is discussed here, along with other measures affecting trade in goods.

We examine the contents of the aforementioned chapters and annexes under six headings: rules of origin; rules for tariff elimination; rules for improving market access; rules for emergency action; standards-related measures; and sectors receiving special treatment.

The NAFTA Rules of Origin

The rules of origin, described in Chapter 4 of the NAFTA, are applied in practice to determine which goods qualify for tariff elimination as they are shipped between NAFTA member countries. Essentially, the free trade provisions of the NAFTA are meant to apply only to goods "originating" in North America. If the NAFTA countries had a common tariff structure on goods produced by nonmember countries, no rules of origin would be required, and all goods could be allowed to circulate duty free among the member countries. The NAFTA is not a customs union, however, but a free trade area and, as such, allows each member country to retain its own tariffs on goods produced outside the area.

An example will help demonstrate why any free trade area like the NAFTA requires rules of origin. Suppose the Canadian tariff on a good produced outside the NAFTA is 10 percent and the US tariff on the same good is 2 percent. In the absence of rules of origin within the NAFTA, a Japanese firm wishing to sell the good in Canada would avoid paying the 10 percent Canadian tariff by shipping to the United States instead, paying the 2 percent US tariff, then shipping duty free into Canada. Rules of origin prevent such trade deflection, which allows external producers to avoid all but the lowest of member countries' external tariffs.

We noted in the preceding chapter the conditions — at least one of which must be met — whereby a good is said to "originate" in North America under the terms of the NAFTA; it is worthwhile to review those conditions once again:

- The good qualifies as "originating" if it is *wholly obtained* in the territory of one or more of the parties (for example, minerals, fish, forest products, vegetables, and so on harvested or extracted in Canada, the United States, or Mexico) or, in the case of a manufactured good, if it is *produced entirely* from such materials in one or more of the NAFTA countries.

- A good produced in the NAFTA area using materials that do not themselves meet a NAFTA rule of origin qualifies as "originating" only if those materials undergo a "substantial transformation" in one or more of the NAFTA countries in the course of the production process. To apply this principle, the three

NAFTA countries agreed on the precise nature of the *changes in tariff classification* that will allow a non-NAFTA, or nonoriginating, material to be considered "substantially transformed."[1] So as not to deny the status of originating good to a product that contains a minimal amount of material that does not meet the required change in tariff classification, the NAFTA introduces a *de minimis* rule. This rule states that a product can still qualify as originating as long as the value of the imported material it contains that has *not* undergone an applicable tariff shift is no more than 7 percent of its transaction value and as long as it satisfies all other NAFTA origin requirements.[2]

- In addition to satisfying the above requirement, or in some cases as an alternative rule, some products must meet a specified *regional value content requirement.*[3] This requirement states that at least 50 percent of the net cost of the good (total cost minus certain specified expenses, such as marketing) or at least 60 percent of its transaction value (reflecting the selling price of the good) must originate in North America.

There are certain key exceptions in the use of these rules, most notably in the automotive and textile and apparel sectors, as well as in the agricultural sector (see the review of exceptions in the section below on "Sectors Receiving Special Treatment").

Marking rules have been developed as required by NAFTA Annex 311. These rules are considered to be "special rules of origin" for determining when a good is considered to be a good of a NAFTA country. The marking rules are used to determine the "country of origin" of a good for the purpose of complying with a requirement

---

1 The "tariff-shift" rules that confer North American origin on products containing imported materials are detailed in Annex 401 of the NAFTA, which, like the GATT, uses the Harmonized System of goods classification.

2 See Jon R. Johnson, *What Is a North American Good? The NAFTA Rules of Origin,* C.D. Howe Institute Commentary 40 (Toronto: C.D. Howe Institute, February 1993).

3 A regional value content requirement is generally imposed where the tariff change rule is viewed as not being sufficient to reflect the degree of substantial transformation required to confer origin.

to mark the good with its country of origin when imported into another NAFTA country.

Tariff Elimination and Customs Procedures

Tariffs

One of the key purposes of any free trade agreement is to eliminate customs duties, or tariffs, on trade among the participants in goods originating within the free trade area.[4]

The tariff schedule established in the Canada-US Free Trade Agreement (FTA) will continue to apply to any goods entering Canada from the United States that meet the *new* rules of origin, *as if Mexico were not included in the free trade area*. In other words, the FTA tariff reduction schedule will continue to apply to goods that originate in the United States and Canada, as well as to goods that have been further processed in Mexico, if that processing has not increased the transaction value of the good by more than 7 percent. For goods entering the United States from Canada, the FTA schedule will apply to any good that satisfies the NAFTA rules of origin, provided it is also eligible to be marked as a product of Canada under the marking rules.

All goods traded between Canada and Mexico or between the United States and Mexico are divided into a number of different staging categories that indicate the rate at which the tariff on a particular good will fall to zero — immediately on some goods; within five to ten years on most, and up to 15 years on others (Annex 302.2).[5] Each country has a lengthy tariff schedule that lists and describes each article traded, and gives for each the current applicable tariff rate and the appropriate staging category.

---

4 For a detailed statement of the NAFTA's tariff provisions, see Article 302 and Annex 302.2.

5 Unless otherwise stated, all parenthetical references in the text are to NAFTA articles and annexes.

As was the case in the FTA, the NAFTA contains a provision that allows for two or more of the signatories to agree on an accelerated tariff reduction schedule. Indeed, the success of this mechanism under the FTA, combined with early requests by industries in the three NAFTA countries, prompted the Canadian government to launch consultations on a first round of early tariff elimination under the NAFTA barely six days after the agreement was implemented.

Customs Procedures

Chapter 5 sets out customs procedures that require importers claiming preferential tariff treatment under the NAFTA to obtain a certificate of origin from the exporter (Article 501), and specifies the manner in which importers and exporters are to use such certificates in dealing with customs authorities (Articles 502–504). There are also provisions for administrative and enforcement measures aimed at preventing the misuse of these certificates (Articles 505–508).

Chapter 5 also addresses the handling of disputes over determinations of the status of particular imports into NAFTA countries as "originating" or "nonoriginating" — in particular, by improving the transparency and harmonization of customs procedures under which the three countries must operate. A common certificate of origin and uniform regulations on the application of rules of origin and customs procedures will be used. As well, the NAFTA contains provisions for advance rulings by customs administrations, and for procedures for reviewing and appealing origin determinations and advance rulings by customs authorities (Articles 509–511). A customs subgroup will provide a forum for the parties to discuss such issues as rules of origin and customs procedures (Article 513).

Other Market Access Measures

National Treatment and Trade Restrictions

The parties to the NAFTA agree to grant one another national treatment as defined in Article III of the GATT (NAFTA Article 301). The

GATT definition of national treatment states that imported products "shall be accorded treatment no less favorable than that accorded to like products of national origin in respect of all laws, regulations and requirements." With respect to provincial or state practices, national treatment means treatment no worse than that accorded to a good coming from a province or state within the same country.

The parties to the NAFTA also agree not to adopt or maintain quantitative import or export restrictions (such as quotas or import licenses) or export and import price requirements (Article 309), except in accordance with Article XI of the GATT. (Article XI permits the use of such measures under certain circumstances; for example, imports may be restricted if the products fail to satisfy domestic standards or regulations, and exports may be restricted if such a measure is necessary to relieve critical domestic shortages.) There are a very limited number of other policies that will also be exempt from this NAFTA requirement; notable among them are Canadian controls over exports of logs and unprocessed fish (Annex 301.3).

In the event that they impose any of the export restrictions permitted under the GATT — for example, in conjunction with restrictions on the domestic production or consumption of exhaustible natural resources — Canada and the United States (but not Mexico) also have a general obligation not to reduce the proportion of the total supply of the restricted good that they make available, on commercial terms, to the other party below the proportion supplied in a recent representative period (Article 315). In the same vein, no NAFTA country may impose export taxes, unless the same taxes are also applied to domestic consumption (Article 314).[6]

Duty Waivers

Effective January 1, 1996 (for Canada and the United States), and January 1, 2001 (for Mexico and the other two parties), the three countries, with very few exceptions, will be limited in their ability to refund paid duties or to waive or reduce duties owed on most

---

6 There are exceptions to this for specified basic Mexican foodstuffs.

nonoriginating goods (Article 303). If such a refund is made conditional on the imported goods' being re-exported or used as material in the production of a good subsequently exported to another NAFTA country (in which case it is referred to as a "duty drawback"), it cannot exceed the lesser of (1) the duty on the good when it was originally imported from a nonmember country on importation into a member country's territory, or (2) the duty paid when it is later re-exported to another NAFTA country.

In addition, the three countries will not be permitted to waive duties based on the fulfillment of a performance requirement, such as preferential purchasing of domestic goods or services or the meeting of domestic content requirements. (Such waivers are called "duty remissions.") There is an important exception to this obligation for Canadian waivers in the automobile sector; the NAFTA is also flexible in the way that Mexico may implement the provision.

Furthermore, if a NAFTA country can show that any waiver of customs duties granted by another NAFTA country to one importer has an adverse impact on the commercial interests of a person from that country or on its economy, then the waiver is either to be terminated or made generally available (Article 304).

Other Market Access Provisions

The NAFTA also contains provisions allowing, under strictly defined conditions, the duty-free entry of goods (regardless of origin) that enter one NAFTA country from another on a temporary basis only. Examples include professional equipment necessary to a business person (who qualifies for temporary entry) to carry out the relevant business activity, and goods intended for display and demonstration (Articles 305–307).

Emergency Action

In merchandise trade between Mexico and the other two NAFTA countries (except in textiles and apparel goods, for which different emergency rules apply), any of the three can temporarily "escape" its obligation to reduce tariffs on its imports from a partner country if those imports result from the NAFTA's trade liberalization, and "constitute a substantial cause of serious injury, or threat thereof, to a domestic industry producing a like or directly competitive good" (Article 801). The injured member country may, under these conditions, suspend any further tariff reduction or even increase the tariff to its pre-NAFTA level (or to the current rate applied to non-NAFTA countries, whichever is less), but only "to the minimum extent necessary to remedy or prevent the injury." As a general rule, the suspension of tariff reductions (or the increase in a tariff) cannot be maintained for more than three years.[7]

Such emergency actions or safeguards are available to the NAFTA countries only during the transition period to the complete elimination of tariffs, and can be taken only once for any particular good from any particular member country. On terminating the action, the country that employed it can either resume the rate of duty that would have applied under the NAFTA had no action been taken or phase out the rate of duty in equal stages, ending on the date specified in the NAFTA for the elimination of the tariff.

Bilateral emergency actions between Canada and the United States, in all sectors but textiles and apparel goods, will fall under the FTA rules, rather than the NAFTA rules (NAFTA Annex 801.1; FTA Article 1101). This means that, between those two countries, only "serious injury," not the "threat" of serious injury, can trigger emergency action. Furthermore, between these two countries, there will be no exceptions to the three-year limit on emergency action.

---

7   Generally, the period of relief can be extended only with the consent of the NAFTA partner against whose good the action is taken. In the case of the few goods for which the tariff is to be phased out within 15 years, however, the relief period can be extended unilaterally for one year. Even in the latter case, the affected industry must be deemed to have implemented a plan of adjustment, and the duty applied during the initial period of relief must be substantially reduced at the beginning of the extension period.

Understanding on Emergency Action

The "parallel accords" on environmental and labor standards signed by the three NAFTA countries on August 13, 1993, were accompanied by an "Understanding on Emergency Action." This is an agreement to establish a Working Group on Emergency Action, which will report to the Free Trade Commission (discussed in Chapter 8 of this book). The working group will serve as a consultation mechanism in the event that one NAFTA country believes that increased imports from another are causing or contributing significantly to serious injury, or the threat of serious injury, to its industry. The working group will also examine trade, productivity, employment, or other economic factors in a particular industry, if requested to do so by a member government and if two of the parties (or two-thirds, if more countries join the NAFTA) agree.

Global Action

Although the NAFTA countries retain their right, under the GATT, to impose global emergency actions — that is, emergency actions that apply to many countries — they must exclude goods from other NAFTA countries from such actions, unless

- imports from a member country account for a substantial share of the imports of the party taking the action (this normally means that the NAFTA country is one of the top five suppliers); and
- imports from the member country contribute significantly to the serious injury, or threat of serious injury, being caused in the affected party by imports (this normally means that the growth rate of imports from the partner in question is not appreciably lower than the growth rate of imports from all sources).

No NAFTA country may undertake a global restriction that affects imports from another NAFTA country without notifying the Free Trade Commission and without ensuring adequate opportunity for consultation with the partner. Moreover, no action is permitted that would have the effect of reducing imports from the partner below the trend established during a previous, representative, period. In any event, if a global action by a NAFTA country does affect one of its partners, that partner is entitled to concessions of substantially equivalent trade effects by way of compensation; if there is failure to agree on such concessions, the partner has the right to retaliate (Article 802).

Standards-Related Measures

Chapter 9 of the NAFTA applies to the internal standards-related measures[8] adopted by the member countries that may, directly or indirectly, affect trade in goods or land transportation and telecommunication services within the free trade area.[9]

The NAFTA recognizes that each member country has the right to enforce on its territory whatever standards it sees fit, even if doing so means prohibiting the importation of a good or service from another NAFTA country that fails to comply with the standard (Article 904). This provision does not interfere with the principle of national treatment for goods imported from a NAFTA partner, since suppliers in the partner country will receive the same treatment as that accorded domestic suppliers.

---

8 "Standards-related measures" refers to standards, technical regulations, and conformity-assessment procedures. The difference between standards and technical regulations is that compliance with the former is not mandatory but compliance with the latter is. Both can refer to product or service characteristics, to the production process for a good or to the operating method in the provision of a service, as they relate to the characteristics of the good or service, or to labeling and other similar requirements. The NAFTA defines a conformity-assessment procedure as any procedure used to determine that a standard or technical regulation is being or has been fulfilled.

9 Chapter 9 of the NAFTA does not cover sanitary and phytosanitary measures, which are dealt with in Chapter 7 of the agreement ("Agriculture and Sanitary and Phytosanitary Measures"), or technical specifications in public sector procurement contracts, which are covered in Chapter 10 of the agreement ("Government Procurement").

In the interest of removing unnecessary standards-related barriers to trade, the NAFTA allows the member countries to try to make their standards more compatible and to increase their mutual recognition of, and fairness in, standards conformity assessment procedures; the agreement also encourages the adoption of international standards in each country (Articles 905–908). Ultimately, however, it is up to each NAFTA country to decide whether or not an imported product meets its standards. (See also Chapter 7 of this book, on environmental and labor standards in the NAFTA.)

According to Article 902, the NAFTA countries must "seek, through appropriate measures," to ensure that the substantive provisions of the chapter on standards-related measures will be observed by state and provincial governments and other standards-setting bodies within their territories, although the precise extent of that obligation has yet to be determined. The three countries must also undertake to provide early notification of any change in technical regulations or other standards or assessment procedures that would be relevant to trade within the free trade area. In addition, each has agreed that, if it allows interested individuals with no government affiliation to be present during the process of standards development in its own country, it will also allow similar individuals from its partner countries to participate (Article 909). To further strengthen these measures, the three countries have agreed to provide one another with "inquiry points," where all their queries can be answered (Article 910).

A Committee on Standards-Related Measures will be set up to monitor progress under this chapter of the agreement — including the progress of various subcommittees and working groups that are looking into specific issues[10] — and to cooperate toward the devel-

---

10 Such groups will include the Automotive Standards Council, which will work toward greater compatibility of national standards-related measures pertaining to automotive goods; the Subcommittee on Labelling of Textile and Apparel Goods, which will work toward such goals as harmonizing the labeling requirements for these goods (for example, by promoting a more widespread use of pictograms); and the Land Transportation Standards Subcommittee and the Telecommunications Standards Subcommittee, which will do comparable work in the area of services.

opment of more compatible standards and enforcement measures (Article 913). The committee will report annually to the Free Trade Commission, and disputes may be referred to it as the first step in the dispute settlement process for standards-related issues.

Sectors Receiving Special Treatment

Agricultural Goods

The NAFTA's agricultural provisions are contained in Chapter 7 of the agreement. This chapter effectively contains three separate bilateral agreements. The Canada-US agreement essentially reflects the status quo of the existing FTA, whereas key elements of Mexico-US agricultural trade are subject to extensive liberalization. Canada and Mexico have also liberalized their agricultural trade to a great degree.

With some exceptions, agricultural tariffs among the three countries will be reduced to zero. Nontariff barriers will be replaced by equivalent tariffs, which will decline to zero over a period of 10 to 15 years. The liberalization of agricultural trade is considered one of the main achievements of the NAFTA. In Canada's case, however, exceptions to this process of "tariffication" are upheld for the supply-managed commodities of dairy products, eggs, and poultry, and Mexico will maintain corresponding restrictions toward Canada (but not toward the United States). These exceptions will likely have to be revised in the light of the December 1993 GATT agreement, whereby Canada agreed to replace its import quotas for supply-managed commodities with very high tariffs that will decline over time.

Canadian tariffs on virtually all other agricultural goods will be reduced in relation to both the United States and Mexico at roughly the same pace that was built into the FTA.[11] Special rules of origin

---

11 For greater detail, see Tim Josling and Rick Barichello, *Agriculture in the NAFTA*, C.D. Howe Institute Commentary 43 (Toronto: C.D. Howe Institute, April 1993); and United States, Congress, Congressional Budget Office, *Agriculture in the North American Free Trade Agreement* (Washington, DC: Congressional Budget Office, May 1993).

and special safeguard rules apply to a class of sensitive agricultural products in each country.

An altogether different section of Chapter 7 of the NAFTA deals with sanitary and phytosanitary measures — that is, measures pertaining to animal and plant health. For the most part, in its general principles, the treatment of these measures mirrors that of other standards-related measures in the NAFTA, as described in the preceding section.

Automobiles

The NAFTA provides special rules of origin for the automotive sector. Annex 300-A ("Trade and Investment in the Automotive Sector") also specifies how the NAFTA will affect a number of the agreements and regulations currently in effect in the automotive sectors of the member countries. These include: the Canada-US auto pact and the automotive provisions of the Canada-US FTA; Mexico's Auto Decree and Maquiladora Decree, as well as its value-added requirements, trade-balancing requirements, and import-licensing measures, as they affect the auto industry; the US corporate average fuel economy (CAFE) regulations; and Canadian and Mexican restrictions on trade in used vehicles.

Annex 300-A begins with two general statements that apply to each of the NAFTA countries:

- with respect to the agreements and regulations mentioned above, no NAFTA country may accord a new producer in its territory better treatment than it accords existing producers, except as specifically allowed in the Annex; and
- the parties will review the working of the Annex and the overall development of the North American automotive sector by the end of 2003, with a view to strengthening its integration and global competitiveness.

With respect to Canada-US trade, the NAFTA essentially confirms that the 1965 auto pact will continue to apply, as it did under the FTA. The FTA rules of origin are, however, replaced by special rules of origin for the automotive sector (Annex 300-A.1, paragraphs 1, 2). The new rules are designed to ensure that the key automotive components of vehicles will have to be sourced in North America for the completed vehicles to be deemed North American and, hence, to benefit from duty-free passage across borders within the NAFTA.

The rules achieve this end in part by imposing a generally higher North American regional content requirement (which must be calculated using the net cost method)[12] for automobiles than for other goods — specifically, 62.5 percent for passenger vehicles, small trucks (for example, minivans), and buses, and 60 percent for tractors, larger trucks and buses, and specialty vehicles.[13] Furthermore, contrary to what is allowed in other sectors in the calculation of regional content, auto producers are not permitted to count as wholly North American an auto part that *would* qualify as such under the NAFTA rules of origin for other goods. Auto producers must instead trace back through their chain of suppliers the exact percentage of key parts and components that is made from imported material, and subtract the value of all such material from their net costs to arrive at the North American content of their vehicle. The NAFTA introduced this requirement in order to avoid the problem of "roll-up" that arose under the FTA, whereby, for example, parts composed of only 50 percent North American content would count as 100 percent North American on being imported into Canada (because they met the 50 percent FTA rule of origin at the Canadian border) and would then be combined with those parts composed of less than 50 percent origin in a final product that would subsequently be exported to the United States. It was possible, in fact, for such products to have less than 50 percent North American content, yet

---

12 This change in the method of calculation means that the new content requirement is not necessarily more demanding in all circumstances, but it typically is.

13 In all these categories, new plants and plants that have been retooled for the introduction of a new model to the North American market will be allowed to meet a modified North American content requirement of only 50 percent for the first five years of operation (for new plants) or two years (for retooled plants).

still meet the FTA rule of origin and enter the United States duty free. Although roll-up is still allowed in other sectors under the NAFTA, it was largely eliminated in the automotive sector because the highly integrated nature of the auto industry in Canada and the United States made it especially open to abuse of this practice.

Of the three countries, Mexico will experience by far the most dramatic changes in its automotive policy as a result of the NAFTA.[14] Mexico has agreed to remove, by January 1, 2004, all the trade-restrictive provisions of its Auto Decree and accompanying regulations, including the requirement that a certain percentage of a manufacturer's total national value added come from "national suppliers";[15] the requirement that, for every dollar of imported parts, a producer must export a certain dollar value in assembled automobiles;[16] and the requirement that a manufacturer must produce in Mexico in order to be allowed to sell there.

Energy and Basic Petrochemicals

As described in the NAFTA's relatively lean Chapter 6, there are few new provisions in the agreement that liberalize trade in energy products very much beyond the substantial liberalization brought about by the FTA. With respect to energy-related trade between

---

14 Those changes are detailed in the 27 paragraphs of Annex 300-A.2.

15 The required value added from national suppliers as a percentage of a manufacturer's total national value added will be 34 percent in 1994–98, declining annually to 29 percent in 2003, then disappearing completely. There is, however, an important exception for manufacturers that produced vehicles in Mexico before the model year 1992. They will be allowed to use the ratio they would have attained in that model year by including purchases from independent maquiladoras that would have achieved national supplier status under the terms of the NAFTA (which caps at 20 percent the ratio of Mexican value added to total sales that Mexico can require of an enterprise, including an independent maquiladora, as a condition of becoming a "national supplier"). Thus, the value-added requirement will disappear more quickly for manufacturers currently established in Mexico than for new ones.

16 Here as well, a "credit" system for meeting past requirements will benefit established manufacturers during the transition period.

Canada and the United States, the provisions of the NAFTA are, for the most part, identical to those of the FTA. An important new provision will require the federal governments of the three countries to put pressure on energy regulatory bodies to dissuade them from disrupting contractual relationships with suppliers in other NAFTA countries.[17]

The NAFTA recognizes the Mexican government's monopoly over the exploration, development, transportation, refining, and sale of petroleum and petroleum products (Annex 602.3). Accordingly, limits will continue to be imposed on trade (and, obviously, investment) in this sector between Mexico and its two NAFTA partners. For example, although the NAFTA would allow Canadian natural gas suppliers to negotiate directly with Mexican firms, any resulting contract would have to be vetted by Petroleos Mexicanos (PEMEX). Furthermore, should Mexico wish to restrict supply to conserve exhaustible resources in the event of a supply shortage or for purposes of price stabilization, it is free to do so without being obligated to make available to the other parties a portion of the restricted supply (which Canada and the United States have to between themselves, as they did in the FTA). Conversely, Mexico does not get the guarantees of access to the US market for energy products that Canada obtained under the FTA, and retained under the NAFTA.

Textiles and Apparel Goods

NAFTA Annex 300-B liberalizes North American trade in textiles and apparel goods in the sense that most quotas and tariffs on goods that meet the rules of origin will eventually disappear (after a long adjustment period with regard to Mexican trade with the other two countries). The rules of origin in this sector are, however, much more stringent under the NAFTA than they were under the FTA. Whereas, under the latter, apparel had to incorporate Canadian or US fabric

---

17 See André Plourde, *Energy and the NAFTA*, C.D. Howe Institute Commentary 46 (Toronto: C.D. Howe Institute, May 1993).

to meet the rules of origin, under the NAFTA's "yarn-forward" requirement, fabric itself (with limited exceptions) must be made from North American yarn. For some cotton goods, the NAFTA rule of origin has an even more demanding "fiber-forward" requirement. As under the FTA, however, textile and apparel makers in one NAFTA country are given substantial quotas up to which they may ship duty free to another NAFTA country without having to satisfy the rules of origin. For Canadian textile and apparel makers exporting to the United States, these quotas are somewhat higher under the NAFTA than they were under the FTA.

Computers, LANs, and Certain Color TV Tubes

The NAFTA requires a certain degree of harmonization in the external tariffs of the three member countries on their imports of computers, local area networks (LANs), and certain color TV tubes from non-NAFTA countries (Article 308 and corresponding annexes). For computers and computer parts, the NAFTA establishes a mini-customs union, in that it requires the relevant Canadian, US, and Mexican tariffs toward non-NAFTA countries to be harmonized to the lowest level applied by any one of them for each item. For LAN apparatus, the three countries have agreed to a common zero tariff toward non-NAFTA countries. This will allow computers, computer parts, and LANs to move duty free within the free trade area without having to meet rules of origin. With respect to certain color television tubes, any NAFTA country contemplating reducing its duties on non-NAFTA imports is expected to consult the other two countries in advance; during the transition period, if the other two are dissatisfied with the decision, they have the right to increase their tariffs on such goods originating *within* the NAFTA.

Wine and Distilled Spirits

With regard to wine and distilled spirits, the NAFTA essentially confirms the FTA's provisions on trade between Canada and the

United States and extends them to trade between Canada and Mexico (Articles 312 and 313, including Annex 312.2). Thus, the NAFTA requires nondiscriminatory listing of wine and distilled spirits based on normal commercial considerations and eliminates discriminatory price markups against the products of another NAFTA country, but allows most other existing discriminatory measures to be retained.

How Does the NAFTA Differ from the FTA and the GATT?

With respect to most aspects of trade in goods, the NAFTA, like the FTA, is inspired by concepts originating in the GATT. In many areas, the NAFTA fleshes out, in terms even more precise than those of the new GATT agreement, how these concepts will apply to trade among the North American countries. This is the case with respect to customs procedures, national treatment, emergency actions, and standards-related measures, among other things.

To cite a specific example, it is the GATT (Article XI) that establishes the principle that an emergency restriction on the supply of an exhaustible natural resource should not result in a reduction of the share that is made available to a trade partner below that which prevailed during a previous, representative period. The FTA and the NAFTA specify *how* this principle is to be applied in energy trade between Canada and the United States.

Indeed, on many issues, such as standards-related measures, the NAFTA previewed the results of the Uruguay Round of GATT negotiations. Moreover, the NAFTA achieved significant liberalization in agricultural trade and trade in textiles, areas that were not even covered under the GATT until the conclusion of the Uruguay Round.

The NAFTA's provisions for trade in goods are in some respects significantly different from the corresponding FTA provisions. With respect to rules of origin, in particular, the NAFTA is clearer and, on the whole, more flexible than the FTA. The NAFTA rules of origin are clearer because much greater precision has been brought to the rules on changes in tariff classification and to the calculation of regional value content. The FTA used a single "50-percent-of-direct-cost" rule for calculating Canadian and US content, which turned out to be subject to different interpretations by the customs authorities of the two countries. Under the NAFTA, not only will fewer goods be subject to the calculation of regional value content, but the methods used for that calculation, together with the publication of uniform regulations by the three countries' customs authorities, are expected to remove much of the ambiguity. For most goods, the NAFTA rules of origin are also more flexible, notably with respect to the *de minimis* rule that exempts the exporter from having to satisfy the change-in-tariff-classification rule of origin if the value of all nonoriginating material is less than 7 percent of the good's transaction value.

For automobiles and textiles and apparel, however, the NAFTA rules of origin are significantly more stringent than the FTA's, particularly with respect to the "tracing" of parts that is required to determine the origin of vehicles assembled in North America, and the "yarn-forward" rule that applies to apparel and textiles.

With respect to computers, the NAFTA goes significantly farther than the FTA, by creating, in effect, a customs union: all the NAFTA countries will apply a single external rate of duty.

The Significance of the Provisions

One of the main consequences of the NAFTA's liberalization of trade in goods is to provide Canadian and US exporters with freer access to the Mexican market. The broader implications of this change are covered in Chapter 10 of this book. Some of the more significant aspects of the NAFTA for exporters, however, are the changes that it effects in the FTA rules governing Canada-US trade.

The changes in the rules of origin brought about by the NAFTA afford all exporters greater certainty as to whether their goods qualify as "originating." This is significant, as some Canadian exporters (particularly smaller ones) found the calculation under the FTA rules so complicated that they chose instead to pay the US duty.

Canada fought the more restrictive NAFTA rules of origin for automobiles because they make access to the US market more difficult for foreign "transplant" automobile producers in Canada, which use a relatively high proportion of imported parts and components. Canada's attempts to attract this form of foreign investment are likely to be hampered in the future by the new rules.[18] Canada similarly opposed the new NAFTA rules of origin for textiles and apparel because they impede access to the US market for Canada's clothing industry, which is dependent on imported yarn.

Some of the positive changes in the NAFTA will, however, mitigate the effects of these increased barriers for the sectors noted above. Among them are higher quotas for duty-free entry into the United States for Canadian-made apparel not meeting the restrictive rules of origin in this sector, an easing of the FTA's duty-drawback prohibition, and greater clarity in the NAFTA rules of origin. The latter will help avoid the kinds of disputes that arose under the FTA as a result of differing Canadian and US customs rulings on rules of origin, the source of the dispute in the well-publicized Honda case in 1992 (which was an example of the roll-up problem). In addition, "transplant" auto producers will benefit from the fact that much more lenient rules of origin will apply to new plants and to plants refitted for models newly introduced to North America.

The effective customs union in computers potentially could become a significant precedent for future trading arrangements in North America and in the entire hemisphere. As Jon Johnson puts it,

> The greatest concern with the NAFTA rules of origin arises from their complexity. After several years of working with the NAFTA rules, the governments of the NAFTA countries may conclude that the most sensible rule of origin in the NAFTA is that which will apply when the mini-customs union for computer goods comes into effect.[19]

---

18 See Lorraine Eden and Maureen Appel Molot, *The NAFTA's Automotive Provisions: The Next Stage of Managed Trade*, C.D. Howe Institute Commentary 53 (Toronto: C.D. Howe Institute, November 1993).

19 Johnson, *What Is a North American Good?*, p. 14.

In other words, success with the mini-customs union could lead to consideration of a comprehensive customs union down the road. However, although a North American customs union would have the advantage of eliminating the need for complex rules of origin within the free trade area, it would also involve potential disadvantages — namely, that the smaller partners in the union would lose control of their individual trade policies to the extent that they would have to adjust their external tariffs to match those of the larger partner; that members would not be able to act unilaterally in reducing tariffs toward nonmember countries; and that the harmonization of tariffs among member countries could actually result in higher barriers against outsiders.[20]

The NAFTA's mini-customs union in computers mostly avoids these pitfalls by harmonizing tariffs for different types of computer equipment to the *lowest* existing level among the NAFTA countries, and by mandating that any reduction in tariffs agreed to by any one NAFTA country at the Uruguay Round of the GATT be adopted by the others. It remains to be seen, however, whether these sound practices could be generalized to a more comprehensive North American customs union.

The NAFTA preserves many of the FTA's most important results for Canada. A notable example is the retention of the provision that each NAFTA country is to exclude the others from any global emergency action it takes against imports.

Despite being only a regional free trade agreement, the NAFTA has many important implications for multilateral trade agreements, particularly but not exclusively in its provisions pertaining to trade in goods. The NAFTA includes significant liberalization of trade in agriculture and textiles, sectors that had long eluded the GATT and other international trade accords. The "tariffication" principle introduced in the NAFTA, whereby quantitative restrictions on agricultural products are replaced by tariffs that must be reduced over time, is one that has usefully been applied in the Uruguay Round.

---

20 Ronald J. Wonnacott, *The NAFTA: Fortress North America?* C.D. Howe Institute Commentary 54 (Toronto: C.D. Howe Institute, October 1993).

The NAFTA is also the world's first comprehensive trade agreement involving both developed and developing countries. In return for free access to the richer markets for its developing industries, Mexico has agreed to forgo the export-subsidizing and import-substituting measures that were central to its trade policies. Notably, with the severe restrictions on duty drawbacks under the NAFTA, Mexico's maquiladora system as it is now known will cease to exist, insofar as Mexico's duties on its non-NAFTA imports used in the manufacture of goods destined for the United States or Canada will be nonrefundable. (It should be added that, once *all* tariffs have been eliminated under the NAFTA, there will be no more duties to refund on imports from the United States or Canada.) In addition, Mexico's agricultural sector — particularly its corn program, which has been called that country's "de facto rural employment and anti-poverty program"[21] — is likely to undergo a tremendous transformation as a result of the eventually free importation of more efficiently produced grain from the United States and Canada. Because of Mexico's position as one of the leading developing economies, these changes can be expected to have a major impact on the future shape of global trade liberalization, beyond the results of the recent Uruguay Round.

Concerns about the Provisions

One general concern about the liberalization of merchandise trade among the NAFTA countries centers on the effects of eliminating trade barriers between an advanced industrial economy, such as that of Canada, and a country with lower wages and effectively lower health and environmental standards, such as Mexico. Although it is often focused on manufacturing industries, this concern cuts across the agreement in general, and is addressed in some depth in Chapters 7, 10, and 11 of this book (dealing, respectively, with environmental and labor standards in the NAFTA, the deal's impact on Canada's economy, and the constraints that the NAFTA imposes on government policy).

---

21 United States, Congress, Congressional Budget Office, *Agriculture in the North American Free Trade Agreement*.

Another set of concerns regarding the NAFTA's provisions on trade in goods applied to the Canada-US FTA as well. Perhaps the most persistent of these is the concern over Canada's alleged obligation to export certain types of goods — specifically, resources such as energy and water — to the United States. This concern has always been unfounded.[22] Canada is *not*, in fact, obligated under the NAFTA (nor was it under the FTA) to make available ever-growing amounts of oil or natural gas to the United States; moreover, it has no obligation to make available any amount at all in the course of normal relations between buyers and sellers. Only if Canada decides to impose supply restrictions under certain circumstances allowed under the GATT must it make available, on commercial terms, to US purchasers a *share* of the restricted supply no smaller than that which prevailed during the 36 months before the restriction was imposed. In other words, the provision in no way threatens Canada's ability to implement, for example, energy conservation policies. It is also worth noting that, in the event of an international oil crisis, Canada is already committed to sharing its oil supplies under the terms of the International Energy Agency agreement.

Any misconception as to the NAFTA's meaning with respect to water exports should by now have been put to rest by the December 1993 statement issued, at the request of the new Canadian government, by the governments of the three NAFTA countries. Among other clarifications, the statement assures that "the NAFTA creates no rights to the natural water resources of any party to the agreement."

A third set of concerns involves the effects that a North American free trade area might have on Canada's future relations with other countries, as well as on the world trading system in general. Are we making the mistake of putting all our eggs in one basket by creating a "Fortress North America" that will shut out trade with the rest of the world and hurt our trading partners outside the United States and Mexico?

---

22 See Richard G. Lipsey and Robert C. York, *Evaluating the Free Trade Deal: A Guided Tour through the Canada-US Agreement*, Policy Study 6 (Toronto: C.D. Howe Institute, 1988), chap. 9.

This question is worth looking at in some depth. When two or more countries liberalize trade between them, they automatically discriminate against countries outside the free trade area by not according them the same preference — specifically, duty-free treatment — that they allow their trading partners within the area. Thus, some of the increase in trade in the newly created area results from one member's "diverting" its import purchases to a partner and away from a lower-cost outside country — an action that damages the outsider. GATT Article XXIV allows free trade areas to be created despite the potential damage to outsiders from trade diversion, provided the participating countries do not raise new barriers against the outside world. The rationale behind this position is that the increased economic growth generated within the free trade area and the consequent increased demand for outsiders' exports may compensate for the negative effects of trade diversion.[23]

It is not clear whether, on balance, the NAFTA effectively raises trade barriers against the outside world. Certainly, in some cases, trade with North America will become more difficult for outsiders. Specifically, in the automobile and apparel and textiles sectors, more stringent rules of origin than those under the FTA mean that auto parts and textile producers outside North America will face greater difficulties in penetrating the market.

With respect to computer equipment, however, the NAFTA reduces barriers against outside countries. Moreover, the clearer and more flexible (except as they pertain to autos and textiles) NAFTA rules of origin are implicitly equivalent to a reduction in trade barriers against outsiders. Finally, as underlined in the next chapter, non-NAFTA residents who have a substantial business presence in one of the NAFTA countries will benefit from the explicit extension to them of the NAFTA's liberalization of trade in services and investment.

---

23 The damage may, at least to some degree, be offset (or more than offset) by increased economic growth generated within the free trade area and the consequent increased demand for outsiders' exports. For more on this issue, see Wonnacott, *The NAFTA: Fortress North America?*

Chapter 5

Services, Investment, and Related Matters

What Does the NAFTA Say?

Services in General

Chapter 12 of the NAFTA applies to cross-border trade in services, excluding financial services and air transportation and related support services (Article 1201).[1] It does not, however, apply to the procurement of services by governments or public sector agencies, which is covered in Chapter 10 of the NAFTA (discussed in Chapter 6 of this book).

The NAFTA states that the principle of national treatment will apply to cross-border trade in services; that is, parties to the NAFTA must give service providers from a partner country treatment no less favorable than that which they accord their own service providers (Article 1202). With respect to provincial and state measures covering the services sector, this provision means that treatment no less favorable than that accorded to out-of-province (or out-of-state) service providers in the same country must be given to service providers from another NAFTA country. In addition, a most-favored-nation (MFN) article prevents NAFTA signatories from giving service providers from any outside country more favorable treatment than that which they accord service providers of a NAFTA country (Article 1203). The NAFTA adopts other liberalizing principles with

---

1 Unless otherwise indicated, all parenthetical references are to NAFTA articles and annexes.

respect to services as well, such as forbidding parties to impose residence requirements on cross-border providers of services from other NAFTA countries (Article 1205).

In practice, however, the application of these principles is subject to numerous exceptions at both the federal and the state or provincial levels. Indeed, special annexes[2] list policies or whole sectors, such as social services, for which any existing measures — and, in a number of cases, future measures — that do not conform to the free trade principles listed above will still be allowed (see Table 2). Specifically, Annex I designates measures existing as of the NAFTA's entry into force that the three countries have chosen to "reserve" — that is, to exclude from the provisions of the NAFTA; Annex II lists sectors in which existing *or* future measures may be reserved. States and provinces have up to two years after the agreement's entry into force to identify any other reservations they wish to add to Annex I. Existing local government measures that might affect cross-border trade in services will not be affected by the agreement (Article 1206).

The three signatories have agreed to list any existing or future quantitative restrictions affecting services that, while they may be nondiscriminatory (and hence do not contravene the agreement's national treatment provisions), might nevertheless constitute barriers to trade. An example of such restrictions is quotas limiting the number of service providers in a given sector. The aim of such identification by the member countries is the eventual liberalization or removal of these restrictive measures as part of future negotiations (Article 1207). In fact, the parties make a commitment to liberalize a limited number of quantitative restrictions, licensing and performance requirements, and other similar measures (Article 1208).

The NAFTA countries have agreed that measures pertaining to the licensing and certification of one another's nationals should be such that they do not constitute an undue restriction on the cross-border provision of services. The agreement also obligates the parties

---

2   These annexes, numbered I to VII, are physically separate from the main text of the agreement and thus, unlike the other annexes in the agreement, are not identified with any particular NAFTA chapter or paragraph.

to eliminate citizenship or permanent residency requirements from the licensing and professional certification of certain categories of service providers from other member countries, and encourages the parties to eventually remove all such requirements (Article 1210). Furthermore, the NAFTA contains provisions that encourage the development of mutually acceptable standards and temporary licensing for a wide range of cross-border providers of professional services (Annex 1210.5).

The benefits of the NAFTA's services provisions will accrue to "service providers of a Party" — that is, to citizens or permanent residents of a member country, or to corporations constituted or organized under the laws of a member country, even if such corporations are controlled by nationals of another (non-NAFTA) country. In certain circumstances, however, the benefits of the services provisions may be denied to non-NAFTA nationals if, for example, the corporation they own or control in a NAFTA country does not conduct "substantial business activities" in the territory of any NAFTA country (Article 1211).

Specific Sectors

Financial Services

NAFTA Chapter 14, on financial services, applies to financial institutions (and investors in financial institutions) of the NAFTA countries and to cross-border trade in financial services (Article 1401). It does not apply to financial activities or services undertaken by or for governments, such as public pension plans.

Providers of financial services in one NAFTA country will have the right, in principle, to establish financial institutions on the territory of another NAFTA country without being subject to requirements (such as ownership requirements) other than those that also apply to domestic financial service providers (Article 1403). In addition, the parties recognize that the following principles apply to trade and investment in financial services between them:

Table 2: *Canadian Policies and Sectors Exempt from the NAFTA's Services and Investment Provisions*

A. Sectoral Reservations

Sector	Derogation	Phaseout
	Annex I	
1. Agriculture	Loans from the Farm Credit Corporation are reserved for Canadians	None
2. Automotive	Waivers on customs duties are linked to performance requirements	None
3. Customs brokerages and brokers	Senior management has nationality restrictions	None
4. Duty-free shops	Ownership of shares and licensing is limited to nationals	None
5. Oil and gas	Production licenses for "frontier lands" and "offshore areas" can be held only by entities that are at least 50 percent Canadian-owned	None
6. Oil and gas	Approval of projects may be linked to technology transfer, domestic R&D expenditures, and local presence	None
7. Oil and gas	"Benefit plans" and technology transfer requirements can be imposed in conjunction with the *Hibernia Development Project Act*	None
8. Uranium	Foreign ownership of a uranium mining property is limited to 49 percent	None
9. Fish harvesting and processing	Foreign vessels are excluded from Canada's Exclusive Economic Zone; the ownership of more than 49 percent of a fish-processing enterprise and the acquisition of a commercial fishing license are mutually exclusive rights for foreign interests	None
10. Air transportation	Domestic air routes and particular scheduled international routes are reserved for firms that are at least 75 percent Canadian-owned	None

Table 2: *Canadian Policies and Sectors Exempt from the NAFTA's Services and Investment Provisions – cont'd.*

A. Sectoral Reservations — continued

Sector	Derogation	Phaseout
	Annex II	
11. Aboriginal affairs	Rights accorded to aboriginal peoples are not subject to any provisions in the NAFTA	[a]
12. Telecommunications[b]	Canada reserves the right to adopt any measures in this area	[a]
13. Securities	Canada reserves the right to adopt any measures with respect to the acquisition or sale of securities issued by any level of government in Canada	[a]
14. Minority affairs	Canada reserves the right to adopt any measures in this area	[a]
15. Social services[c]	Canada reserves the right to adopt any measures in this area	[a]
16. Air transportation	Canada reserves the right to adopt any measure that restricts foreign ownership of specialty air services to 25 percent or less	[a]
17. Water transportation	Canada reserves the right to adopt any measures in this area	[a]
18. Water transportation	This is a tit-for-tat reservation in response to a US reservation	[a]

Table 2: *Canadian Policies and Sectors Exempt from the NAFTA's Services and Investment Provisions — cont'd.*

B. All-Sector (Rules-Based) Reservations

Derogation	Phaseout	Particular Features
Annex I		
1. Review procedures and some performance requirements that may be required under the *Investment Canada Act* are excluded from the agreement	None	
2. The federal and provincial governments maintain the right to limit the ability of foreign interests to acquire assets or equity interests in state enterprises when such assets are being sold or otherwise disposed of	None	Not subject to freeze on future discriminatory measures — that is, structured like an Annex II reservation
3. The ownership of shares in federally incorporated corporations may be constrained	None	
4. A "simple majority of the board of directors, or of a committee thereof, of a federally- incorporated corporation must be resident Canadians"	None	
5. Non-Canadians' ownership of land in Alberta may be limited	None	
6. Foreign ownership of seven companies involved in air transportation, energy, and high technology is restricted	None	
Annex II		
7. Any measures can be adopted with respect to the ownership of oceanfront land	[a]	

[a] Phaseouts do not apply to Annex II, which specifically lists reservations that allow for future increases in discriminatory treatment.

[b] Telecommunications transport networks and services, radio communications, and submarine cables.

[c] Includes the following services, to the extent that they are established or maintained for a public purpose: income security (or insurance), social security (or insurance), social welfare, public education, public training, health, and child care.

Source: Michael Gestrin and Alan M. Rugman, *The NAFTA's Impact on the North American Investment Regime*, C.D. Howe Institute Commentary 42 (Toronto: C.D. Howe Institute, March 1993), with some modifications by the authors.

- freedom for nationals of and persons located in one NAFTA country to purchase financial services from providers in another NAFTA country;
- national treatment (treatment no less favorable than that accorded the domestic financial services industry);
- MFN treatment (treatment no less favorable than that accorded financial services providers of any other country); and
- freedom to transfer information for processing.

In addition, governments cannot require that more than a simple majority of the boards of directors be composed of nationals or residents of the NAFTA country in which their operation is located (Articles 1404–1408).

As is the case with services and investment in general, the liberalizing principles listed above are subject to numerous reservations maintained by the three countries' federal governments. Those reservations are listed in Annex VII (Article 1409). Provinces and states may also list their reservations in this annex. Moreover, there is no restriction on the right of NAFTA signatories to adopt or maintain measures for prudential reasons, such as protecting depositors or the stability of their financial systems (Article 1410).

Mexico made important reservations that will retain market-share limitations for certain institutions until 2000. The limitations will apply, both in aggregate and on the size of individual operations, to Canadian and US banks, securities dealers, and insurance companies (as well as to similar non-NAFTA firms incorporated in Canada or the United States). US and Canadian factoring and leasing companies, however, will not face a limitation on the size of their individual operations other than a temporary limit on the aggregate presence of all such companies in Mexico; other financial institutions, as well as joint ventures between Canadian or US and Mexican insurance firms in which control remains in Mexican hands, will be free of limitations as soon as the NAFTA comes into effect.[3]

---

3 See Pierre Sauvé and Brenda González-Hermosillo, *Implications of the NAFTA for Canadian Financial Institutions*, C.D. Howe Institute Commentary 44 (Toronto: C.D. Howe Institute, April 1993).

The NAFTA's financial services chapter also provides for a dispute settlement mechanism (Articles 1414 and 1415) inspired by but separate from the agreement's general dispute settlement process. It is described briefly in Chapter 8 of this book.

Telecommunications

Chapter 13 of the NAFTA, which contains provisions on telecommunications, ensures that nationals of a member country are able to access and use (but not provide) public telecommunication transport networks or services in another NAFTA country. Nationals of member countries are allowed to provide a wide range of other services, such as interconnecting private circuits to public telecommunications networks, on whatever conditions they wish to make them available (Articles 1301 and 1302). The agreement also liberalizes the provision of value-added telecommunication services in one NAFTA country by firms based in another, whether or not the service is provided across national borders (Chapter 12 and Article 1303).

Land Transportation

Mexico's Annex I provides that the restrictions on cross-border transportation by truck, bus, or rail to and from points in Mexico that currently apply to Canadian and US nationals will be removed within three to six years. This will mean, for example, that a Canadian trucker can deliver Canadian goods to the United States, then pick up goods there for delivery anywhere in Mexico. Such transports must, of course, observe the regulations that are in force within each country. The agreement covers only cross-border transportation, not cabotage (the transport of goods entirely within a country).

Cultural Industries

Except for the elimination of customs duties on goods that may have cultural content, any Canadian measure affecting cultural industries will be governed by the rules established in the Canada-US Free Trade Agreement (FTA). The result is that the measure will be exempt from the NAFTA, and another government will have the right to retaliate only if the measure otherwise contravenes the FTA (Annex 2106).

Movement of Business Persons

Chapter 16, on the temporary entry of business persons from one NAFTA country into another, essentially builds on the pioneering provisions of the FTA. The earlier agreement greatly facilitated business travel between Canada and the United States for specified categories of professionals (such as accountants, social workers, computer systems analysts, and teachers) performing certain types of services (such as research, sales, or after-sales services) or conducting investment activities. These provisions have now been extended to Mexico, although the United States reserves the right to limit entry of such business persons from Mexico to 5,500 a year during the first ten years of the agreement's implementation.

Investment

Chapter 11, the NAFTA's investment provisions, affirms that the principles of national treatment and MFN status apply to the treatment of investors — and their investments — from one NAFTA country in another (Articles 1101 and 1102). With respect to any investment on its territory (including investments by nationals of non-NAFTA countries), the NAFTA forbids the imposition of certain performance requirements, including requirements to export specified amounts of goods or services, to achieve given levels of domestic content, transfer technology,[4] or to act as exclusive supplier for the

---

4 An important reservation listed in Annex I states, however, that "Canada may impose requirements, or enforce any commitment or undertaking...for the transfer of technology, production process or other proprietary knowledge to a national or enterprise, affiliated to the tranferor, in Canada, in connection with the review of an acquisition of an investment under the *Investment Canada Act*." See also Table 2, in this chapter.

regional or world market. There are exceptions to this general pro-hibition: foreign investors *can* be subjected to certain performance requirements when they take advantage of export promotion and foreign aid programs, or in the context of certain public procurement contracts.

In addition, any advantages, such as subsidies, granted to specific investments must not be conditional on requirements for the purchase of domestic goods, on required domestic content levels, on import restrictions linked to the foreign exchange inflows generated by the investment, or on domestic sales restrictions linked to foreign exchange earnings. (Again, the first two of these prohibitions may not hold in the case of export promotion and foreign aid programs and certain public procurement contracts.) However, the NAFTA explicitly allows any advantages granted to an investor to be condi-tional on the location of a particular investment, on the provision of a particular service, on the training or employment of workers, on the construction or expansion of a particular facility, or on a commit-ment to conduct research and development activities (Article 1106).

There are numerous reservations to these liberalizing principles (Article 1108). Reservations contained in Annexes I and II of the NAFTA (including reservations listed by states and provinces) will apply to the agreement's investment provisions as well as to services. In addition, in Annex III, Mexico lists the 11 sectors that are reserved for ownership exclusively by the Mexican state, most notably the energy sector. In Annex IV, the NAFTA parties list treaties to which they are signatories that run counter to the MFN provisions of the investment chapter, as well as areas in which they reserve the right to negotiate such treaties in the future.[5] (These are treaties by virtue of which the NAFTA governments give better treatment to investors from non-NAFTA countries than they accord investors from other member countries.)

---

5 For an explanation of these reservations, see Michael Gestrin and Alan M. Rugman, *The NAFTA's Impact on the North American Investment Regime*, C.D. Howe Institute Commentary 42 (Toronto: C.D. Howe Institute, March 1993), pp. 5–6.

Notable among these exceptions is Canada's retention of its right to screen direct investments above a threshold initially set at C$150 million and recalculated annually for investments originating in either the United States or Mexico. Canada also retains the right to waive customs duties for auto producers meeting the requirements of the 1965 auto pact. As in the case of services, although the intent of the investment provisions is to ensure that new measures affecting investment in any NAFTA country conform to the agreed-on provisions, they nonetheless allow member countries not only to maintain existing nonconforming measures in some areas, but even to include new federal reservations in the areas listed in Annex II (see Table 2). This is the case, for example, with respect to restrictions on the acquisition by nonresidents of firms that are being privatized, and to any measure affecting minority affairs, social services, and water transportation.

The NAFTA requires that any expropriation by one member country of an investor from another member country be made for a public purpose only, in accordance with due process of law, on a nondiscriminatory basis (observing the national treatment principle), and on payment of fair compensation (Article 1110). As in the case of services, the benefits of the NAFTA's investment provisions may also accrue to corporations owned or controlled by non-NAFTA interests. The latter may, however, be denied the benefits of the NAFTA's investment provisions under certain circumstances — notably, if they do not conduct "substantial business activities" in any of the NAFTA countries (Article 1113).

The agreement provides for a dispute settlement mechanism specific to disputes between an investor from one NAFTA country and the government of another NAFTA country (Articles 1115–1138). This important section of the NAFTA's investment chapter is described in Chapter 8 of this book.

Competition Policy

A small but important chapter of the NAFTA, Chapter 15 requires each signatory to maintain an effective competition policy, although this requirement is not subject to the agreement's dispute settlement provisions. The parties also agree to cooperate and coordinate to make enforcement in this area more effective (Article 1501). At the same time, however, the NAFTA states that nothing in the agreement prevents a member country from maintaining or designating a government monopoly, as long as, in so doing:

- it does not introduce new trade barriers — such as import and export licenses — that are inconsistent with the provisions of the agreement;
- it treats foreign investors and suppliers on the same footing as domestic ones with respect to the purchase or sale of the monopoly good or service; and
- it does not use its monopoly position to hurt an investment or investor of another NAFTA country in a nonmonopolized market — for example, through the discriminatory provision of the monopoly good or service.[6]

The same provisions will apply to any privately owned monopoly designated by a NAFTA country after the agreement enters into force.

In the same vein, the NAFTA explicitly states that the establishment of a state enterprise by a member country does not run counter to the agreement, provided that the enterprise does not discriminate in the sale of its goods or services against investors or investments of another NAFTA country and that it exercises any authority delegated to it by the government in conformity with that government's obligations under the investment and financial services chapters of the NAFTA (Article 1503).

Intellectual Property Rights

Chapter 17 requires its signatories to help nationals of other NAFTA countries protect and enforce their intellectual property rights by, at

---

6 These provisions do not apply to public sector purchases.

a minimum, giving effect to a number of international agreements in this regard (Article 1701) and according nationals of other NAFTA countries national treatment with respect to such protection and enforcement.[7] The member countries may implement more extensive intellectual property rights than those required by the NAFTA (Article 1702) or, conversely, they may limit such rights to the extent that they have an adverse effect on competition (Article 1704). Specific provisions apply to such intellectual property as compilations of data, sound recordings, computer programs, encrypted program-carrying satellite signals, copyrights, trademarks, patents, trade secrets, and industrial designs (Articles 1705–1713). On patents, the NAFTA countries are required to provide at least 20 years' protection from the filing date, or 17 years' protection from the patent's grant date (Article 1709). The obligations set forth in the intellectual property chapter will, however, generally apply only to acts occurring after the NAFTA comes into effect (Article 1720).

How Does the NAFTA Differ from the FTA and the GATT?

Until 1995, when the new Uruguay Round agreements come into force, the General Agreement on Tariffs and Trade (GATT) will not apply to trade in services, investment, or intellectual property. Neither will it apply, even after 1995, to the movement of business people.

On services, a new General Agreement on Trade in Services, like the NAFTA, spells out a general obligation by the signatories to accord national treatment (and most-favored-nation treatment) to providers of certain types of services from other parties to the agreement. This provision would, however, be subject to a list of exceptions spelled out by each member country. Annexes on financial services and telecommunications would contain some of the basic obligations, but not all of the detailed ones, that are found in the NAFTA.

---

7 Except in the case of sound recordings, for which the NAFTA allows reciprocity of treatment instead of national treatment.

On investment, the new GATT agreement calls for the elimination of measures that are inconsistent with the principles of national treatment and the prohibition of quantitative restrictions, a provision that already applies to trade in goods. For example, parties would be forbidden, as they are by both the FTA and the NAFTA, to require foreign investors to perform a certain amount of local procurement. The text of the draft Final Act of the GATT on intellectual property was essentially reproduced in the NAFTA.

The main conceptual difference between the NAFTA and the FTA in the services area lies in their approaches to identifying sectors as covered or not covered by the liberalization. The FTA required the principles of free trade, particularly that of national treatment, to apply to all future measures taken by governments in sectors that were specified by the agreement — in other words, it provided a list of "covered" services. Thus, by definition, existing measures that derogated from free trade were "grandfathered" in the FTA, and whole sectors were excluded from the scope of the agreement. The NAFTA, by contrast, proclaims a general liberalization of trade in services *except* where the federal, provincial, and state governments have listed "reservations" that exempt specific sectors or types of measures. (A limited number of these reservations involve a phase-out period.) Because of its guiding principle in the area of services — "if it is not specified, it is covered" — the NAFTA liberalizes more broadly than did the FTA, which was guided by the opposite principle — "if it is not specified, it is *not* covered."

On the movement of business persons, the NAFTA's provisions are essentially the same as those of the FTA; the liberalizing measures contained in the latter are simply extended to Mexico, albeit subject to some initial restrictions on numbers.

Many of the NAFTA's investment provisions — and the general thrust of the investment chapter — build considerably on those of the FTA. Like the FTA, the NAFTA affirms that the national treatment principle applies to the treatment of investors from one NAFTA country — and of their investments — in another NAFTA country. Like the FTA, the NAFTA requires that any expropriation of an investor of another party to the agreement be made for a public purpose only, in accordance with due process of law, on a nondiscriminatory basis (observing the national treatment principle), and on payment of fair compensation.

There are also significant differences, however, between the FTA's and the NAFTA's investment chapters. The FTA's national treatment provisions applied only to *new* measures affecting investment; it did not apply to service sectors that were not explicitly covered by the agreement. In contrast, following the model applied to services, the NAFTA's liberalization is granted to *all* investors and their investments, existing and new, except in the sectors and policies explicitly *excluded* in annexes to the agreement.

In addition, the NAFTA's provisions extend to a broader group of investments than do those of the FTA. For example, the NAFTA covers commercial real estate and the equity and debt securities of an enterprise, whereas the FTA applied essentially to direct investments. The NAFTA also spells out in greater detail provisions designed to protect international investors and their investments. These include extending NAFTA protection to non-NAFTA investors who have "substantial business activities" in one NAFTA country and wish to expand into another, and a dispute settlement procedure allowing recourse to binding international arbitration.

The list of forbidden performance requirements is longer in the NAFTA than in the FTA. However, the NAFTA does allow for certain types of performance requirements in some cases — notably, as mentioned, those involving export promotion and foreign aid programs or public sector procurement.

Intellectual property essentially was not covered by the FTA, so its inclusion in the NAFTA is an innovation.

The Significance of the Provisions

It has increasingly been recognized that, unless trade in services is liberalized, the advantages of merchandise trade liberalization cannot be fully realized. Business services such as sales and transportation are critical to getting the goods to customers, while efficient telecommunications and financial services, for example, are critical to the competitiveness of manufacturing production.

Although the NAFTA's chapters on services and investment spell out general liberalizing principles, the practical impact of the agreement on the services sector and on investment flows cannot be understood without the annexes that provide the exceptions to the liberalization. Furthermore, it must be remembered that the cornerstone of the liberalization is not a harmonization of standards (as it is, for example, in the European Union) but national treatment — that is, the right of each country to impose any law or regulation it wishes, provided it does not thereby discriminate against services providers or investors from another member country.

Like the FTA, the numerous NAFTA annexes have the practical effect of retaining key restrictions on services and on US investments in Canada. Services sectors that were exempt in the FTA — for example, those related to health, social services, cultural industries, and basic telecommunications — will continue to be exempt from the NAFTA provisions. However, services trade with Mexico is liberalized under the agreement, notably in the business services sectors (for example, financial services and telecommunications) in which Canada is competitive.

Financial services are treated on the model of general services to the extent that the basic liberalizing provisions are superseded by exceptions that preserve much of the status quo between Canada and the United States; there is, however, a significant opening with respect to opportunities in Mexico. The NAFTA's failure to achieve immediate access to the US market for the Canadian financial services industry must be ranked as a disappointment, as it was with respect to the FTA. By virtue of the national treatment principle, combined with the fact that the Canadian financial services market is much more liberalized than the US market, US financial services firms will continue to have greater leeway to operate in the Canadian market than vice versa.

Nonetheless, the NAFTA's inclusion of general liberalizing principles in the financial services area, inspired by the GATT discussions on a General Agreement on Trade in Services, and the fact that disputes involving the financial services industry are now subject to a slightly modified version of the NAFTA's general dispute settlement mechanism, should be seen as an improvement, in the long run, over the piecemeal liberalization achieved under the FTA. The NAFTA's institutional approach is expected to encourage the eventual harmonization of treatment of the financial services industry across North American jurisdictions and, ultimately, to lead to equal competitive opportunities for the Canadian industry, which remains restricted in its US operations by the traditional national treatment concept.[8]

The provisions pertaining to the temporary entry of business persons should benefit Canadian exporters of both goods and services.

As in the case of services, the NAFTA's obligations pertaining to investment impose virtually no new constraints on Canada: existing investment review rules continue to apply, and continue to be outside the jurisdiction of the deal's dispute settlement mechanism. Similarly, key sectors that were exempt under the FTA continue to be exempt. The extension of the investment chapter's coverage to most forms of "passive" investment is straightforward for Canada, and the international arbitration procedures for investor-state disputes are spelled out in recognition of Mexico's different judicial and administrative processes. (This is true for many provisions of the agreement that set standards of dealings between governments and the private sector.)

Clearly, the NAFTA's extension of FTA rules to Mexico will encourage direct investment in that country; it will perhaps even cause a redirection to Mexico of investment that would otherwise have come to Canada. Had Canada refused to join the NAFTA, however, Mexico would simply have entered into a bilateral trade agreement with the United States — or could even have applied the rules unilaterally — to the same effect. Being powerless to prevent this development, it was in Canada's interest to respond in a way

---

8 See Sauvé and González-Hermosillo, *Implications of the NAFTA.*

that would maintain its attractiveness to investors by securing equal access to the growing Mexican market and maintaining a competitive position in the US market. The NAFTA is a good instrument with which to achieve this end.

Most investors and services providers from nonmember countries that are established in a NAFTA country will be able to benefit from the agreement's liberalization measures on services and investment. This should increase the attractiveness of every NAFTA country, including Canada, for foreign businesses wishing to serve the North American market.

Because Canada's economy is becoming increasingly information based, Canadians in general are likely to benefit from the NAFTA's inclusion of intellectual property rights. Protecting proprietary rights to information makes good business sense for an economy such as Canada's. Many developing countries were not enthusiastic about extending such rights through the GATT because they are net importers of information and want to be able to obtain it at the lowest possible price. By contrast, because Canada aims to be a net exporter of art, patents, designs, computer programs, and other kinds of intellectual property, it must ensure that the associated rights are protected in order to receive a fair price for its exports. Moreover, strengthening intellectual property rights should lead to greater overall investment in intellectual property, and hence in such endeavors as scientific research.

Concerns about the Provisions

The NAFTA's provisions on services, investment, and related matters give few causes for concern beyond those already encountered in the FTA[9] because they largely preserve the numerous exemptions established under the FTA.

9　The concerns that were raised with respect to the FTA are surveyed and answered in Richard G. Lipsey and Robert C. York, *Evaluating the Free Trade Deal: A Guided Tour through the Canada-U.S. Agreement*, Policy Study 6 (Toronto: C.D. Howe Institute, 1988), chaps. 14, 16. Many of the concerns center on the issue of sovereignty, which we also address in Chapter 11 of this book.

Although the United States, unlike Canada or Mexico, does not exempt investment review procedures from the chapter's general liberalization provisions, it does reserve the right to apply national security criteria in a number of areas, including investments by nationals of other NAFTA countries. Since the NAFTA specifically excludes measures relating to national security and they are not ordinarily subject to challenge under the agreement, this gives the United States a *potentially* wide berth should it want to exclude Canadian and Mexican investors from participating in such endeavors as, say, high-technology consortia with US defense companies. From the Canadian point of view, this represents an important flaw in the investment chapter.[10]

Some observers have expressed the concern that obligations under the NAFTA in the area of intellectual property will make it more difficult for Canada's generic drug industry to reproduce foreign pharmaceuticals at low cost. It must be noted, however, that the extended patent protection stipulated in the NAFTA is consistent with both recent changes in Canadian domestic policy on patent protection for pharmaceuticals and intellectual property provisions in the recent GATT agreement.

Finally, with respect to the continued protection of Canada's cultural industries, the NAFTA's provisions on intellectual property rights should cause no renewed concerns. Annex 1206 states that, notwithstanding any other provisions of the NAFTA, any measure regarding cultural industries will be governed exclusively in accordance with the FTA.

---

10 See Gestrin and Rugman, *The NAFTA's Impact on the North American Investment Regime.*

Chapter 6

Government Procurement

What Does the NAFTA Say?

Amounts and Sectors Covered

Government procurement — the purchase, lease, or rental of goods and services by government entities and by certain public sector enterprises — is covered in Chapter 10 of the NAFTA. The aim of the provisions is to make public sector procurement by the three participating governments more accessible to businesses located in all NAFTA countries.

The chapter begins by listing the government entities (such as departments) and enterprises (such as publicly owned agencies or corporations) covered by the provisions, which apply to contracts for certain types of goods, services, and construction work that exceed specified threshold values (Article 1001).[1] The threshold values on contracts awarded by the federal government entities referred to are US$50,000 for goods and services other than construction — although the US$25,000 threshold established in the Canada-US Free Trade Agreement (FTA) will continue to apply between those two countries — and US$6.5 million for construction services contracts. The thresholds on contracts awarded by the public sector agencies and corporations referred to are US$250,000 for goods and services and US$8 million for construction contracts. The threshold values will be adjusted every two years for inflation, as registered by the

---

1 Unless otherwise indicated, all parenthetical references are to NAFTA articles and annexes.

US Producer Price Index for Finished Goods, and translated into Canadian dollars and Mexican pesos at the exchange rate that prevails, on average, during those two years.

The provisions do not apply to all public procurement of goods. Exceptions for Canada include shipbuilding, urban rail and transportation equipment, and communications equipment. Many types of goods purchased by the military in all three NAFTA countries are also exempt from the agreement.

Similarly, the provisions do not cover all procurement of services. The most significant exceptions are transportation services, even if such services are included as part of a procurement contract for goods that *is* covered by the agreement; public utilities services; research and development services; and — with respect to Canada only — education, health, and social services. In addition, the provisions for construction procurement apply only to the list of construction services specified in the NAFTA.

Furthermore, Mexican procurement contracts that are financed by loans from regional and multilateral financial institutions are not subject to the NAFTA procurement provisions, "to the extent that different procedures are imposed by such institutions (except for national content requirements)." Mexico is obligated to open up procurement by PEMEX and CFE (the state-owned petroleum and electrical monopolies, respectively), as well as all government procurement of construction services, but only gradually over a ten-year period. Some procurement funds set aside for small and minority businesses in Canada and the United States are exempted from the agreement, and Mexico has reserved the right to similarly exempt some portion of its public sector contracts. Furthermore, unless and until provincial public utilities in Canada are brought under the terms of the NAFTA procurement chapter, only Mexican and US businesses will be allowed to bid on US power authority contracts under the terms of the NAFTA.

Except for these important exceptions, businesses in any NAFTA country will generally enjoy equal access to the procurement activities, above the specified threshold amounts, of the government departments and agencies listed in the agreement. This freer access to government procurement is in most cases also granted to enterprises controlled by nationals of nonmember countries if those enterprises conduct "substantial business activities" in a NAFTA country.

Evaluation of Bids and Awarding of Contracts

The NAFTA contains provisions concerning the proper valuation of contracts, to guard against such practices as breaking up the value of a contract into smaller components to avoid exceeding the threshold value (Article 1002). Further, in the bid evaluation phase, the parties are forbidden to evaluate bids on the basis of offsetting factors such as local content, technology licensing, or investment (Article 1006), or to require technical specifications or seek technical advice with the purpose of creating obstacles to trade (Article 1007). In particular, government entities must specify their needs in terms of performance criteria rather than a particular design or trademark.

The NAFTA seeks to ensure that the tendering of contracts proceeds in a way that does not discriminate against or otherwise preclude competition among suppliers located in the NAFTA countries (Article 1008). Accordingly, there are guidelines on: the nondiscriminatory qualification of suppliers; the information that must be provided in invitations to participate in bids; where to publish that information; fair procedures for tendering by invitation; fair time limits for the tendering of proposals and for the delivery of the contracted goods or services; the content and handling of the tender documentation provided to suppliers; and disciplines on contract negotiations and on the opening of tenders and awarding of contracts (Articles 1009–1015).

In some circumstances, government entities of NAFTA countries will be allowed to use limited tendering procedures — that is, to contact suppliers individually — provided this is not done to avoid competition or to protect domestic suppliers. Limited tendering would be allowed, for example, if the good or service could be supplied only by a particular supplier and if no reasonable alternative or substitute existed; if a case of extreme urgency occurred or if exceptionally advantageous purchasing conditions arose; if the entity wished to procure a limited amount of a new good or service produced in the course of research, an experiment, a study, or original development (Article 1016); or if the entity needed to procure consulting services of a confidential nature. Government entities covered by the agreement are expected to prepare a report on any contract awarded under such circumstances, for use as needed to exchange information or for the settling of disputes.

Exempt Policies

The procurement chapter explicitly *does not* prevent the NAFTA countries from adopting measures to protect public morals, order, or safety; human, animal, or plant life or health; or intellectual property. They are free to adopt measures relating to goods or services produced by handicapped persons, philanthropic institutions, or prison labor — they are free, for example, to ban imports of goods or services produced by prison labor. They may also take any action, or choose not to disclose any information, related to the procurement of military supplies or other procurement deemed indispensable for national security or national defense purposes, if they consider such a course of action necessary for their essential security interests (Article 1018).

Challenge of Bid Procedures

The NAFTA allows suppliers to challenge bid procedures for procurement contracts covered by the agreement (Article 1017). These challenges are to be reviewed expeditiously by a national authority that has "no substantial interest" in the outcome of the procurement. In some cases, the reviewing authority may even delay the awarding of the proposed contract pending resolution of the challenge, and entities targeted by the challenge normally have to follow the recommendations of the reviewing authority on how to resolve the issue.

The reviewing authority is able to recommend changes in the procurement procedures of the entity being challenged, to the extent that those procedures do not conform to the terms of the NAFTA. This recourse is available not only to suppliers of one NAFTA country wishing to challenge the bid procedures of another, but also to suppliers wishing to challenge the procurement practices of their own government.[2]

The NAFTA governments are requested to make available to one another and to one another's suppliers information on their procurement procedures in general and specific contracts in particular, including an annual statistical report on contracts awarded (Article 1019), as well as information concerning their procurement training and orientation programs (Article 1020).

A Committee on Small Business was established to promote government procurement opportunities for small businesses (Article 1021). Furthermore, the NAFTA mandates negotiations, to begin within five years of the agreement's entry into force, to expand the coverage of the government procurement chapter and to include under its terms, on a voluntary and reciprocal basis, state and provincial government entities (Article 1024).

How Does the NAFTA Differ
from the FTA and the GATT?

With respect to coverage, the NAFTA expands on the FTA's chapter on government procurement and on the 1979 Code on Government Procurement of the General Agreement on Tariffs and Trade (GATT). Whereas the FTA essentially reproduced the list of government entities covered under the GATT code, the NAFTA adds some key Canadian and US entities — notably, the Canadian departments of

---

2 Indeed, similar FTA provisions were frequently used in this way by Canadian businesses. See Christopher Nicholls, *Government Procurement and Canada-US Trade*, Ontario Centre for International Business Working Paper WP 1992-49 (Toronto: Ontario Centre for International Business, 1992).

Communications, Transport, and Fisheries and Oceans,[3] the Royal Canadian Mint, Canadian National Railways and Via Rail, the US Departments of Energy and Transportation, and the US Army Corps of Engineers.[4]

The NAFTA's coverage of services procurement, including many construction services, represents a very significant expansion over the previous coverage, since neither the 1979 GATT procurement code nor the FTA addressed this sector. And since Mexico is not a signatory to the GATT procurement code, the NAFTA obviously opens up entirely new opportunities in the Mexican public sector for Canadian and US exporters. Furthermore, the FTA made no reference to future negotiations to extend its coverage to state and provincial entities, as the NAFTA does, or to special efforts to expand procurement opportunities for small businesses.

There are also important differences between the NAFTA and the FTA with respect to procedures for awarding procurement contracts covered by the agreement. The NAFTA's provisions regarding limited tendering give governments more flexibility than they had under the FTA to avoid cumbersome tendering procedures, when these can be shown to impede the efficiency of government (just as they might impede the operation of a private business). The NAFTA, however, strictly limits the criteria governments may use to assess bids: they must focus on issues of technical specifications, rather than basing their evaluations on perceived benefits in terms of, for example, domestic content.

In December 1993, multilateral negotiations on government procurement, which paralleled the Uruguay Round negotiations, resulted in a new GATT Agreement on Government Procurement. A salient feature of the new code is that it establishes detailed guidelines for bidding and tendering procedures and for awarding contracts, and puts in place a procedure for challenging bids that resembles the

---

3 The NAFTA's procurement provisions will *not* apply to certain office equipment and specialized machinery procured by these three departments.

4 Heavy electrical equipment procured by the Army Corps of Engineers is exempted from the provisions.

procedure outlined in the NAFTA. Another key innovation in the new GATT agreement is that, like the NAFTA, it covers public sector purchases of services, and construction contracts. The new GATT code will, however, apply only to contracts valued at amounts far above the NAFTA thresholds — for example, US$176,000 for purchases of goods and services by government. Moreover, Mexico is still not one of the 12 signatories to the GATT code.

The Significance of the Provisions

From the point of view of business' gaining greater and fairer access to the government procurement markets of the member countries, the NAFTA constitutes an improvement over both the FTA and the GATT. Not only will Canada and the United States gain significant new access to contracts awarded by the Mexican public sector, they will also benefit from expanded access to each other's markets. According to both Canadian government and US private sector estimates, the value of procurement contracts accessible to Canadian companies under the NAFTA will be C$70 billion (in today's dollars) by 2003, compared with the C$20 billion that would have resulted had the arrangements under the 1979 GATT code and the FTA prevailed.[5] Even then, however, the continued exemption of subnational governments and many types of federal procurement means that only about 10 percent of public sector procurement in North America will fall under the NAFTA rules.

Indeed, with regard to procurement by state and provincial entities, the NAFTA negotiators were able to provide only for further negotiations. Thus, these governments are still free to maintain

---

5 The C$50 billion difference includes C$30 billion in US government-procured services and US$1.5 billion from the lifting of "Buy America" restrictions on rural electrification loans. The US Chamber of Commerce estimates that total procurement by the Mexican government is currently US$18 billion. Canadian suppliers of electrical, oil and gas, telecommunications equipment ,and building materials, as well as consulting engineers and high-technology software providers are expected to benefit from access to that market.

significant obstacles to cross-border procurement; for example, most of the "Buy America" restrictions applied by US state and local governments remain in force, continuing to pose a significant obstacle to Canadian companies vying for government contracts south of the border.

The NAFTA had a positive impact on the recent GATT negotiations on government procurement, which achieved many of the results obtained in the NAFTA, including extended coverage (for example, to services contracts) and improved dispute settlement procedures. In addition, the NAFTA has showed that it is indeed possible to bring developed and developing countries together in a trade-liberalizing agreement on public sector procurement, an achievement that still eludes the GATT.

Concerns about the Provisions

Some analysts are concerned about the constraints that international agreements put on the procurement practices of signatory governments. According to one view, the purpose of government procurement is not only to provide the public sector with required goods and services at the most advantageous price possible, but also to be used as an instrument of public policy — for example, to create employment during times of high unemployment and to sustain it throughout the business cycle in poorer areas of the country.[6]

Ultimately, however, government spending designed primarily to sustain employment in certain industries or regions often has an effect opposite to the one desired, and can also have undesirable side-effects. Industries sustained by government contracts that are not challenged by normal competition tend not to be as innovative and cost-conscious as other industries or firms, and they become less

---

6 Indeed, according to this view, the government, as a rational consumer, may in fact be better off by imposing a premium on bids from nondomestic firms in times of high domestic unemployment, since it can expect to collect additional taxes from work performed domestically. See Nicholls, *Government Procurement and Canada-US Trade*.

competitive in the long run as a result. The situation might be described as one of investing public money — and often encouraging the investment of private money — in the past rather than the future. Also, when the cost of public sector purchases is higher than it need be,[7] the public gets inferior value for its money, which results in a higher tax burden on the economy as a whole. Consequently, procurement practices that are not internationally open may reduce national welfare instead of increasing it.

Another major impact of this sort of procurement is that it tends to reduce opportunities for exporters. Countries are opening up their public sector procurement markets to foreign competition only on a reciprocal basis. Thus, for Canada to keep its own market closed would likely spell trouble for its export performance — and, hence, for export-related employment — which has come increasingly to rely on markets in nontraditional areas, including that of foreign public sector procurement. International agreements on government procurement are clearly meant to prevent this outcome by mandating that firms from all signatory countries must be allowed to compete on an equal footing with national firms. This openness should increase welfare in the same way that reducing trade barriers in the private sector would.

Some observers argue, however, that the sweeping nature of agreements on public sector procurement could in fact result in *less* efficient decisionmaking. Although it is true, the argument goes, that everyone benefits from the added transparency of the system, the rigid tendering requirements that characterize such agreements do not allow for the development of networks of reliable suppliers or permit the channeling of contracts toward suppliers that come up with innovative products tailored to the purchaser's needs — two practices that are common in the private sector.

Some critics also contend that governments should be free to encourage, through strategic purchases, the development of fledg-

---

7   Often because it includes, directly or indirectly the lobbying and other rent-seeking activities of both the winning and the losing bidders.

ling domestic companies or products that show promise of becoming viable in the long run but are unable initially to overcome steep barriers to entry into the world (or domestic) market.

The NAFTA's recognition of some of these concerns is evident in its exemption of certain areas, such as research and development contracts, from the provisions on services procurement and, especially, in its allowance of limited tendering under circumstances where that would clearly be the more efficient option. Ultimately, however, the benefits of the NAFTA's reciprocal liberalization of public sector procurement will come from the reduced ability of governments to award contracts on the basis of considerations other than cost and performance and from the increased access that exporters will gain to other NAFTA markets.

Chapter 7

Environmental and Labor Standards

What Does the NAFTA Say?

Treatment in the Agreement

Environmental concerns are given more prominence in the NAFTA than in any other international trade agreement, including the General Agreement on Tariffs and Trade (GATT) and the Canada-US Free Trade Agreement (FTA). The following summarizes the NAFTA's key environmental provisions, which are scattered throughout the various chapters of the agreement:

- The NAFTA states that specific obligations set out in certain international environmental and conservation accords to which one or more of the NAFTA countries are signatories take precedence over the NAFTA in the event that the latter conflicts with the former (Article 104).[1]

- The NAFTA in effect recognizes the right of the three parties to adopt any standards-related measures toward "legitimate objectives," such as any level of protection of human, animal, or plant life or health; protection of the environment; or consumer protection (Article 904).[2]

---

1 Unless otherwise indicated, all parenthetical references are to NAFTA articles and annexes.

2 This is subject to the obligation by the NAFTA countries to avoid arbitrary or unjustifiable distinctions between similar goods or services in the level of protection...

- The NAFTA explicitly recognizes that a member country, in enforcing a standards-related measure, may refuse to allow the entry of products from another party that do not conform to the measure (Article 904), unless the exporting party can show, in dispute settlement, that the measure is an unnecessary obstacle to trade. A measure can be found to be such an obstacle when it has not been demonstrated that its purpose is to achieve a legitimate objective *and* when it operates to exclude goods from another country which satisfy that legitimate objective (Article 914).

- Any efforts, undertaken as part of the agreement, to achieve greater compatibility and equivalence of standards-related measures should in no case result in less stringent standards on the environment, the protection of life or health, and consumer safety (Article 906). In other words, any harmonization of environmental, health, or safety standards and regulations among the three parties will be made toward the most stringent standard, not the least stringent one.

- A NAFTA signatory must notify the other parties of any new or modified technical regulation that it proposes to adopt. A copy of the measure must be made available to any interested person who requests it, and such persons must be allowed to make comments in writing, which the party proposing the measure must be prepared to discuss and to take into account. Similar requirements apply to standards and conformity assessment procedures. NAFTA parties must also seek to ensure that state and provincial governments abide by these rules (Article 909).

- Anything a party does to ensure that investments on its territory are undertaken in a manner sensitive to environmental concerns — such as requiring environmental reviews of investment

Note 2 - cont'd.

...they consider appropriate — for example, by discriminating between similar goods or services for the same use, under the same conditions that pose the same level of risk and provide similar benefits (Article 907).

projects — is not to be construed as contravening the NAFTA's investment liberalization provisions (Article 1114), although any such measure must otherwise still be consistent with the NAFTA's investment provisions.

- It is "inappropriate" for a NAFTA signatory to relax domestic health, safety, or environmental measures in order to attract investment (Article 1114). The NAFTA contains no mechanism to enforce this admonition, however — only a provision for consultation.

- In the same vein, notwithstanding the obligation to provide patent protection to inventions in all fields of technology, a party may prohibit the granting of patents that might cause serious damage to nature or the environment (Article 1709).

- If a measure in one NAFTA country aimed at protecting the environment or human, animal, or plant life or health is challenged by another NAFTA country in a dispute that arises under both the GATT and the NAFTA, and if that dispute raises factual issues concerning the environment, health, safety, or conservation, the country complained against can choose to have the matter settled under the NAFTA's dispute settlement rules rather than through the GATT (Article 2005).

Except for a statement in the preamble to the effect that the three parties are resolved to "improve working conditions" and "protect, enhance and enforce basic workers' rights,"[3] the NAFTA is silent on the subject of labor standards other than those subsumed under health and safety standards.

---

3 Article 1603 states that a party may refuse to authorize employment by a business person of another party if that person's temporary entry — which would otherwise be permitted under the NAFTA's provisions on temporary entry for business persons — might adversely affect a labor dispute in the place of employment or the employment of any person involved in such a dispute. This is, in a sense, an anti-strikebreaker clause applying across the NAFTA boundaries.

The Parallel Accords on Environmental and Labor Standards

US President Bill Clinton launched negotiations in early 1993 toward agreements on the environment and labor standards that would be "parallel" to the NAFTA. In doing so, he was fulfilling a promise made during the 1992 presidential campaign, when he said that he could support the NAFTA, negotiated by the then-incumbent Bush administration, only if agreements on environmental and labor standards were negotiated with Canada and, in particular, Mexico. The North American Agreement on Environmental Cooperation and the North American Agreement on Labor Cooperation, concluded on August 13, 1993, are the outcome of those negotiations.[4]

Agreement on Environmental Cooperation

The North American Agreement on Environmental Cooperation seeks to ensure that the signatories enforce the environmental legislation applicable within their territory. It also commits each signatory to maintain high levels of environmental protection and to strive to continually improve legislation to that effect.

In addition, the agreement establishes a Commission for Environmental Cooperation, comprising a governing Council, a Secretariat, and a Joint Public Advisory Committee. The Council will consist of cabinet-level representatives of the parties and will meet at least once a year or whenever a signatory to the agreement requests. The Council will be responsible for future environmental cooperation among the NAFTA countries on issues such as the environmental impact of proposed projects with significant transboundary effects and the protection of endangered species.

---

4 Clinton also requested that negotiations take place with Canada and Mexico on the threat of import "surges" following trade liberalization. Those negotiations resulted in the "Understanding on Emergency Action" that accompanied the two agreements on the environment and labor. This document was described briefly in the section entitled "Emergency Action" in Chapter 4 of this book.

Besides supporting the work of the Council in a technical sense, the Secretariat will consider submissions by any person or non-governmental organization alleging a signatory's failure to enforce its environmental laws effectively, and will seek factual information and a response regarding such allegations. The Joint Public Advisory Committee will be made up of five members of the public from each country. Its role will be to advise the Council and provide any relevant information to the Secretariat.

The agreement also provides for a dispute resolution mechanism to deal with trade-related environmental disputes between governments. The mechanism can be invoked if a party is alleged to be guilty of a "persistent pattern of failure to effectively enforce an environmental law." The situation in question must relate to the production of goods or services traded between the parties. Should the Council be unable to resolve the dispute, an arbitral panel may then be set up at the request of the complaining party or parties, but only if two-thirds of the countries agree.

Arbitral panels are to be selected from an agreed-on roster of environmental and other experts. If a panel finds that a country has persistently failed to enforce its environmental legislation, the parties involved in the dispute have 60 days to agree on an action plan to remedy the situation. If no such agreement occurs, the panel may evaluate the action plans proposed by the party complained against, then devise a plan of its own and determine fines ("monetary enforcement assessments") to be imposed against the government in question. Fines may not exceed US$20 million in the first year of the agreement; in subsequent years, that limit is to be adjusted in line with the growth of trade in the free trade area. In any event, a fine must be imposed if the action plan devised by the panel is not fully implemented. Fines collected must be used by the Council "to improve or enhance the environment or environmental law enforcement" in the country that has paid the fine. If the government against which the complaint has been directed fails to pay the fine or continues not to enforce the relevant environmental law, then the complaining party may invoke enforcement procedures.

The enforcement procedures for Canada differ from those for the other NAFTA countries. If Canada is the party complained against, the Commission for Environmental Cooperation may go before a Canadian court to collect the fines or enforce the required action plan. If another country is the party complained against, the complaining country or countries may suspend NAFTA benefits — that is, reverse or suspend trade barrier reductions imposed by the NAFTA — by an amount equivalent to the required fine.

Another objective of the agreement is greater transparency and cooperation on environmental matters among the parties. It seeks to achieve this goal by requiring the parties to undertake such measures as reporting on the state of the environment, promoting the use of economic instruments to achieve environmental goals efficiently, and ensuring appropriate private access to procedures for the enforcement of environmental laws.

Agreement on Labor Cooperation

The North American Agreement on Labor Cooperation strives to monitor and strengthen the enforcement of labor laws in each of the NAFTA countries and to solve labor-related trade issues. In certain cases, the levying of fines and, with respect to Mexico or the United States, the use of trade sanctions will be permitted in the event that disputes cannot be resolved. Through this agreement, the parties commit themselves to promoting principles such as freedom of association, the right to collective bargaining, restrictions on child labor, the elimination of discrimination in employment practices, the right to compensation for injuries incurred in work-related accidents or for occupational diseases, and the protection of migrant workers. The agreement commits the parties to effective enforcement of their respective labor laws on these and other issues and to ensuring open access by interested persons to the administrative, judicial, and other tribunals with jurisdiction over these matters.

The agreement creates a Labor Commission, comprising a Ministerial Council (composed of the labor ministers of the signatory countries), which is to supervise the implementation of the agreement; an International Coordinating Secretariat, which is to play a technical support role in addition to gathering and publishing information on labor issues in all three countries; and National Administrative Offices (NAOs) in each country, which will serve as points of contact for the exchange of information required by the agreement. The NAOs are to become involved when questions related to the enforcement of labor laws arise between member countries and require joint consultation. If questions cannot be resolved at that stage, a party may request consultations at the ministerial level to resolve the issue. The ministers may at that stage call upon an *ad hoc* Evaluation Committee of Experts to help in their discussions, unless a party obtains a ruling by an independent expert that the matter under review is not trade related or is not covered by mutually recognized labor laws. The committee of experts is called on to analyze patterns of practice in each country on the subject and to present a report to the Ministerial Council.

If these mechanisms fail, if a dispute concerns a member country's alleged persistent pattern of failure to effectively enforce labor laws with respect to health and safety, child labor, or the minimum wage, and if the situation involves mutually recognized labor laws and touches on the production of goods or services traded between NAFTA countries, any party may then request that an arbitral panel be established. The panels are to be composed of experts on labor and other matters, who are to be jointly selected. The dispute settlement mechanism on labor-related trade issues then proceeds exactly as in the case of environment-related trade disputes, described in the preceding section.

Extent of the Obligations

An important potential exemption for Canada from both parallel accords stems from the role and jurisdiction of the provinces in setting labor and environmental policy. Thus, with respect to the agreement on environmental cooperation, the provinces have to declare their willingness to be bound by it in their areas of jurisdiction. The Canadian government cannot act for the benefit of a province that has not declared itself bound by the agreement, and neither can another NAFTA country bring cases against such a province. Furthermore, the Canadian government cannot bring cases against a NAFTA partner in areas that, in Canada, are under provincial jurisdiction, unless provinces accounting for at least 55 percent of Canada's gross domestic product have agreed to be bound *and* unless at least 55 percent of production in the affected industry or sector takes place in provinces that have agreed to be bound. Reciprocally, other NAFTA countries cannot bring cases against Canadian provinces in such industries or sectors.

Similarly, under the agreement on labor cooperation, unless at least 55 percent of the workers in the industry or sector affected by a complaint are located in provinces that have agreed to be bound by the agreement, cases cannot proceed against Canada in areas of provincial jurisdiction, and neither can Canada initiate cases against other NAFTA countries.[5]

How Does the NAFTA Differ from the FTA and the GATT?

The GATT recognizes that any measure taken by one of its contracting parties that is "necessary to protect human, animal or plant life and health" is justified, even if it restricts trade, provided that it does not constitute a "means of arbitrary or unjustifiable discrimination between countries where the same conditions prevail, or a disguised restriction on international trade" (GATT Article XX[b]). The same applies for any measure "relating to the conservation of exhaustible natural resources," provided these measures are not simply export

---

5 For more detail on the interaction between the NAFTA and environmental and labor issues, see William G. Watson, *Environmental and Labor Standards in the NAFTA*, C.D. Howe Institute Commentary 57 (Toronto: C.D. Howe Institute, February 1994).

restrictions but also involve restrictions on domestic production or consumption (GATT Article XX[g]).

The FTA's chapter on technical standards states that standards-related measures that are implemented to achieve a "legitimate domestic objective" and that do not "operate to exclude goods of the other Party" are not to be seen as unnecessary obstacles to trade (FTA Article 603). A "legitimate domestic objective" was defined as an objective "whose purpose is to protect health, safety, essential security, the environment, or consumer interests."

Thus, the texts of the GATT and the FTA already provide a degree of support for the right of countries to adopt standards and other policies toward broadly defined "legitimate objectives," provided that their intent is not to dampen cross-border trade.

Although the NAFTA is consistent with these two trade agreements, it makes the exemptions in favor of environmental and other standards-related measures clearer, and expands the list of possible exemptions to include such objectives as "sustainable development." Moreover, where factual issues are raised, the NAFTA explicitly allows far greater input by environmental experts and organizations, input that will be taken into account in the formulation of panel decisions as to whether a standards-related measure constitutes an improper trade restriction. And, with the strengthening of the dispute settlement mechanism contained in the NAFTA (see Chapter 8 in this book), NAFTA panel decisions seem to stand least as good a chance of being implemented than do GATT decisions. Finally, the NAFTA goes beyond the GATT and the FTA by allowing input by environmental groups and other interested parties from one NAFTA country into the formulation of standards-related measures by another. The parallel accords on the environment and labor issues create, in effect, a trilateral mechanism giving a party to the agreement the right to seek the imposition of sanctions or fines against another party that repeatedly fails to enforce its own domestic environmental and (in certain areas) labor laws. In contrast, the GATT and the FTA allow trade sanctions only if a signatory reneges on its obligations under those agreements.

The Significance of the Provisions

The extent to which international trade agreements can affect the environment and the impact of environmental regulations on trade have been the subject of growing concern and policy debate. Environmental or social "dumping" — that is, one country's retention of labor or environmental practices that are not tolerated in other countries in order to attract production or investment away from those countries — is decried not only for potentially leading to greater pollution and social inequality in the host country, but particularly because it could result in a "downward harmonization" of standards to the lowest common denominator across the free trade area. However, the possibility that regulations purported to protect the environment will act as disguised trade barriers is seen as a serious problem by both developing countries and small trading countries, such as Canada. Left unchallenged, such barriers would give governments in large countries, such as the United States, the ability to impose their own standards on the smaller ones. Pressures to avoid such problems were clearly present as the NAFTA negotiators began their work, and their impact is equally clear in the agreement itself and, of course, in the parallel accords.

The NAFTA is a significant landmark on the road to integrating trade and environmental concerns. The participating governments were determined from the outset to preserve and even strengthen their right to impose any environmental and other standards-related measures according to their respective priorities. Indeed, under the NAFTA, the member countries have left themselves considerable latitude to implement their chosen level of protection (or their own definition of sustainable development) through environmental, safety, and other standards. Such standards will run afoul of the trade agreement only if a complaining party is able to show that they constitute unnecessary obstacles to trade. By placing the burden of proof on the complainant, the agreement ensures that, in specific trade disputes involving the environmental regulations of a given country, environmental concerns will receive full recognition.

Furthermore, the NAFTA dispute settlement process is somewhat more disposed to favoring environmental regulations than is that of the GATT, in the following ways:

- the party complained against can require that a matter arising under both trade pacts be dealt with through the NAFTA dispute settlement process;
- the NAFTA is clearer than the GATT in its recognition that environmental regulations and other standards should not normally be considered barriers to trade or investment;
- the NAFTA dispute settlement process formalizes giving weight to scientific evidence in trade disputes; and
- NAFTA panel recommendations must normally be adopted, whereas GATT panel reports can be blocked indefinitely —albeit only until the new GATT agreement comes into effect in 1995.

The NAFTA parallel accords also allow for verification that environmental and certain labor standards are being appropriately enforced in a NAFTA country, and allow sanctions to be taken if that is found not to be the case. Furthermore, through its inquiry points and notification and transparency provisions, the NAFTA allows any interested person from a member country to be apprised of and have input into any new environmental or other regulation of another NAFTA country.

Concerns about the Provisions

The NAFTA provisions seem to address in a straightforward manner the legitimate concerns of Canadian and US citizens that trade with Mexico will open the door to products that do not meet the health, safety, and environmental standards that they have defined for themselves. For many, however, it is not sufficient that countries be allowed to enforce product-related standards on their own territory, as the NAFTA stipulates. Rather, they should also be able to dictate the enforcement of process-related standards in another country by, for example, refusing entry to goods that, although they may meet domestic product standards, were produced abroad by a *process* that would not be approved domestically. As already noted, in addition to the concern about increased pollution in the country that has lower standards, some fear that the NAFTA, by removing obstacles to imports of Mexican products into the United States (and, as a somewhat secondary consideration, into Canada), will encourage a "downward harmonization" of North American environmental and labor standards.

To what extent is this fear valid — that is, to what extent is free trade between countries with different standards likely to lead to a downward harmonization of those standards? It is true that, by respecting each country's right to set the standards it wants, the NAFTA does not prevent a member country from harboring more polluting production processes than those in place in another. Potentially, this would give firms an incentive to move to or establish themselves in the country with the most lax enforcement of environmental or labor regulations — Mexico, in the case of the NAFTA. Polluting economic activities would then simply be removed from US and Canadian soil, and transposed to Mexico. However, it is unlikely that this effect would involve more than a few marginal cases. Even for relatively footloose firms, the "advantages" of being able to operate with less stringent environmental restrictions are not large — at least, not large enough, in the vast majority of cases, to offset other competitive considerations. If they were, Canada and the United States would have felt tremendous pressure before now to downgrade their standards, since the duties they have imposed on Mexican products in recent years have been fairly low. Indeed, the opposite effect seems to be occurring, in that Mexico is feeling significant pressure to upgrade its standards. Moreover, Canada currently trades — and is willing to sign multilateral trade agreements — with many countries that have even lower environmental and labor standards than Mexico, without suffering an exodus of its industries to these locations.

To the extent that it does exist, the Mexican "advantage" in this regard would likely wane over time because Mexican standards of living are expected to rise as a result of free trade, and rising living standards typically generate demands for less polluting production processes. In any event, the main concern with Mexican environmental regulations involves not their scope, but their enforcement. Thus, in 1992, two opponents of the NAFTA stated:

> Mexico's environmental rules, on the books, are already similar to those in the United States. Indeed, one Mexican regulation requires any manufacturer located within 100 kilometres of the US border to abide by US [Environmental Protection Agency] standards as well as any additional standards adopted by the contiguous US state. The problem is lack of enforcement on the part of SEDUE, Mexico's environmental agency. Of over 600 maquiladora plants in Tijuana, only seven have had their SEDUE applications approved; operation is not contingent on receiving approval.[6]

As we have seen, the parallel accords to the NAFTA allow Canada and the United States to retaliate commercially in the event that Mexico is repeatedly found not to enforce its environmental or labor regulations, a measure that is likely to encourage Mexico to step up its efforts in these areas.

Indeed, many of the NAFTA provisions can be expected to have the net effect of raising environmental and other technical standards in all the NAFTA countries. As mentioned, there are provisions that require standards to be harmonized "upward" rather than "downward" in the event that such harmonization is agreed on. This requirement has very real implications for the work of various standards-related subcommittees and working groups, such as the Land Transportation Standards Subcommittee, which will seek to achieve compatibility in standards relating to, among other things, the transportation of dangerous goods.

---

6 Jeff Faux and Richard Rothstein, *Fast Track, Fast Shuffle: The Economic Consequences of the Administration's Proposed Trade Agreement with Mexico* (Ottawa: Canadian Centre for Policy Alternatives, April 1991), p. 14.

Furthermore, the NAFTA's removal over time of the special incentives that resulted in the cluster of maquiladora plants along the US-Mexican border will help to ease the problem of cross-border pollution between Mexico and the United States. And, although increased Mexican output and the increased volume of transportation between the two countries could potentially exacerbate cross-border environmental problems, the United States and Mexico have agreed to increase funding to clean up the border areas at the same time that the NAFTA takes effect.

As noted earlier, some observers have suggested that Canada should have the right to block Mexican products that, while meeting Canadian product standards, are made using processes that pollute Mexico's environment. But we must bear in mind that such a provision, in the context of the NAFTA, would give the United States the right to block Canadian products on the same grounds. Because many of Canada's exports are based on natural resources, many Canadian producers could be left exposed to US protectionist actions disguised as environmental measures. Some Canadian firms are already concerned about their apparent inability to fight off the negative effect of US standards on their US sales.

Some Canadians believe that the NAFTA should go even farther by allowing Canada to force Mexico to adopt more stringent environmental and labor standards. An objection analogous to the one just described applies here as well: Canada cannot set up an enforcement mechanism that would apply only to foreign policies and standards, and not to its own. Any principle of extraterritorial jurisdiction within the free trade area would have to embrace *all* member countries. This would jeopardize the ability of Canada's federal, provincial, and local governments to determine the level of environmental, labor, and other protection appropriate to their respective jurisdictions because it would make them subject to US and Mexican interests.

In a bilateral or multilateral environmental agreement, of course, trade sanctions could be used to enforce standards *to which the parties had mutually agreed.*[7] We believe, however, that the NAFTA adequately deals with any plausible environmental threat that might arise from this particular agreement and, indeed, goes as far as it can to deal with trade-related environmental concerns without exposing Canada to the threat of having its environmental agenda set by other countries.

---

7 On this point, see Ronald J. Wonnacott, "Canadian Trade Policy for the 1990s," *Policy Options* 14 (July-August 1993).

Chapter 8

Institutions and Dispute Settlement

What Does the NAFTA Say?

Chapter 20 of the NAFTA provides for overarching institutions to ensure the smooth functioning of the agreement, and contains a mechanism for settling disputes stemming from varying interpretations of the agreement. The NAFTA also includes other settlement procedures for specific types of disputes. Most notable among these are the provisions in Chapter 19 that apply to antidumping and countervailing duty cases; the provisions in Chapter 11 for the settlement of disputes between investors and governments and the provisions in Chapter 14 on disputes involving the financial services sector. We will examine these various mechanisms in turn.

Institutions

Chapter 20 begins by setting up institutions that will oversee the overall functioning of the NAFTA, including its dispute settlement mechanisms. The chapter establishes a Free Trade Commission, which will consist of cabinet-level representatives of the parties to the agreement, or their designates (Article 2001).[1] The commission will have a broad role to play in ensuring the smooth functioning and future evolution of the NAFTA. In particular, it will be a key mechanism for helping to resolve disputes concerning the interpre-

---

1 Unless otherwise indicated, all parenthetical references are to NAFTA articles and annexes.

tation and application of the agreement, and it will supervise the work of all committees and working groups established under the agreement. The commission will convene at least once a year in regular sessions chaired successively by each of the parties to the agreement. A Secretariat, comprising sections in each member country, will provide assistance to the commission, particularly with respect to the work of dispute settlement panels and all other committees or groups operating under NAFTA provisions (Article 2002).

General Dispute Settlement under the NAFTA

Grounds for Calling on the Dispute Settlement Mechanism

The parties are entreated to reach consensus on the interpretation of the agreement, and to strive to resolve any matter affecting the operation of the agreement through cooperation and consultation (Article 2003). Should this approach fail, a party may avail itself of the NAFTA's dispute settlement procedure, on the grounds that an actual or proposed measure of another party is inconsistent with the obligations of the agreement[2] or otherwise causes the nullification or impairment of benefits that could reasonably be expected to accrue from the NAFTA (Article 2004).[3] The Free Trade Commission becomes involved at an early stage to try to solve the dispute, but if it is unsuccessful, the dispute settlement procedure calls for the establishment of arbitral panels. The parties to the dispute will

---

2 Except with respect to disputes pertaining to financial services and antidumping and countervailing duties, which are subject to a separate mechanism.

3 The use of the NAFTA's dispute settlement procedure on grounds of "nullification and impairment" of benefits is limited to benefits that can derive from the agreement's provisions on (1) trade in goods; (2) technical barriers to trade; (3) trade in services (except telecommunications, where the telecommunications chapter is inconsistent with the chapter on services in general, and financial services); and (4) intellectual property.

normally be expected to adhere to the recommendations of the arbitral panel (see Table 3).

If a matter arises under both the NAFTA and the General Agreement on Tariffs and Trade (GATT), a complaining party may choose to have it settled at the GATT (Article 2005). However, the party that is the subject of the complaint may request that the dispute be settled instead solely through the NAFTA under the following conditions:

- if it declares that the disputed action was taken to conform with one or more of the specific international environmental obligations listed in the NAFTA; or
- if the dispute arises under either the Chapter 7 provisions on sanitary and phytosanitary measures or the Chapter 9 provisions on standards-related measures, and involves measures adopted by a party to protect its human, animal, or plant life, health, or the environment, and raises factual issues regarding the latter.

Once the parties have settled on one forum, recourse to the other is prohibited.

Composition of Arbitral Panels

Panels established under Chapter 20 must be composed of five individuals with experience in law, international trade, international trade dispute resolution, or other matters covered by the NAFTA; be independent of any signatory government; and comply with a code of conduct established by the Free Trade Commission. To help in the selection of these panels, the commission maintains a roster of up to 30 individuals who meet these criteria and whom the commission appoints by consensus, for renewable three-year terms (Article 2009). Panelists will normally, though not necessarily, be selected rom this roster. An individual who has already been called on by the commission to give expert advice on a particular dispute may not serve on the arbitral panel assembled to resolve that dispute (Article 2010).

Table 3: *The NAFTA's Dispute Settlement Timetable*

Number of Days From: Consultation/ Establishment of Panel	Action
0^a	A party may request consultations on an actual or proposed matter.
30^b	If the parties fail to resolve the matter, either party may request a meeting of the Free Trade Commission.
40	The commission is to meet.
70/0	Either party may request the establishment of a panel.
77/7	A third party may join as a complaining party.
$85/15^c$	The parties are to agree on the chair of the panel.
100/30	Each disputing party is to select two panelists who are citizens of the other party.^{d}
110/40	The complaining party files its initial submission.
130/60	The party complained against files its countersubmission. A third party files its initial written submission.
139/69	The participating parties provide the Secretariat with the names of the persons who will be attending the hearing.
144/74	The panel holds a hearing.
$145/75^e$	After this date, neither a party nor the panel may request a written report from a scientific review board.
154/84	The parties file supplementary written submissions.
190/120	The panel issues its initial report.
204/134	The parties provide written comments to the panel on its initial report.
220/150	The panel presents its final report to the parties.
	The disputing parties present the final report, including a scientific review board report and written views that a disputing party wishes to append, to the commission.^{f}

Table 3 - *Notes and Source*

[a] Article 2006(4) provides that consultations on matters regarding perishable agricultural goods are to commence within 15 days of the request.

[b] Under Article 2007(1), a party may request a meeting of the commission within: (a) 45 days of a request for consultations if another party has subsequently requested or participated in consultations on the same matter; or (b) 15 days of a request for consultations in matters regarding perishable agricultural goods.

[c] Article 2011 provides that, if the disputing parties do not agree on the selection of a chair, the party chosen by lot shall select the chair within five days and the timetable will be adjusted accordingly. If there are more than two disputing parties and the parties do not agree on the chair, the disputing party or parties on the side of the dispute chosen by lot shall select the chair within ten days.

[d] If there are two complaining parties, the party complained against shall select two panelists — a panelist who is a citizen of one complaining party and a panelist who is a citizen of the other complaining party. The complaining parties shall select two panelists who are citizens of the party complained against.

[e] The panel, or disputing party, can request a written report of a scientific review board on factual issues concerning environmental, health, safety, or other scientific matters. The review board report shall not be requested any later than 45 days before the date on which the initial report is due. Time periods are suspended until the disputing parties have filed written objections to the review board report, which occurs 74 days after the request for a scientific review board report.

[f] Chapter 20 does not specify the date on which the parties are to forward the final report to the commission. The final report is to be published 15 days after its receipt by the commission, unless the commission decides otherwise.

Source: Canada, Department of External Affairs and International Trade.

The chair and other members of the panel are selected according to elaborate rules (Article 2011). A key feature of these rules is that a party to the dispute cannot choose its own nationals as panelists. Instead, it selects the two nationals of the *other* party or parties to the dispute who will sit on the panel ("reverse selection").[4] Similarly, if the parties cannot agree on a chair for the panel, one party, selected by lot, must choose a chair who is not one of its citizens — indeed, the chair need not be a national of a NAFTA country.

Resolution of Disputes

The NAFTA states that, as a means of dispute resolution, the removal of the offending measure is preferred, wherever possible, to compensation to the complaining party (Article 2018). The parties are expected, under normal circumstances, to observe the arbitral panel's recommendations. If no resolution of the dispute occurs within 30 days of the parties' receiving the panel's final report, the complaining party may take measures that have an effect equivalent to that of the offending measure — that is, the NAFTA allows the complainant to retaliate against the offending party (Article 2019).

Constraints on Domestic Proceedings

The NAFTA further provides that, in the event that an issue of interpretation or application of the agreement arises in the course of domestic judicial or administrative proceedings in a NAFTA country, the issue must be submitted to the Free Trade Commission, which will endeavor to agree on an interpretation. If it manages to do so, its interpretation will be submitted, through the government of the NAFTA country in question, to the particular domestic court or administrative body undertaking the proceedings (Article 2020). If

---

4 At least two of the panelists will be nationals of the party complained against, even if there are more than two disputing parties — that is, more than one complaining party.

not, any party may submit its views to the court or tribunal. This being said, a complaint by private parties in one NAFTA country claiming that a measure of another NAFTA country is inconsistent with the agreement cannot be dealt with by domestic courts; rather, it must be addressed according to the terms of the NAFTA's dispute settlement procedures (Article 2021).

Settlement of Private Commercial Disputes

With regard to commercial disputes between private parties in the free trade area, the agreement encourages the use of arbitration and other means of alternative dispute resolution, and to this end establishes an Advisory Committee on Private Commercial Disputes (Article 2022).

Antidumping and Countervailing Duties

Continued Application of Trade Remedy Laws

Each party reserves the right to apply its antidumping and countervailing duty laws to goods imported from the territory of any other party (Article 1902). The parties also reserve the right to change or modify their antidumping and countervailing duty laws, although such amendments must not be inconsistent with the GATT or with the "object and purpose" of the NAFTA, and will apply to goods of another party only if so specified in the amendment. With respect to such changes, the amending party must notify as far as possible in advance any party to which the amendment applies, with a view to allowing the latter sufficient time to initiate consultations regarding the changes.

In addition, a party may request that another party's modifications of its antidumping or countervailing duty laws be referred to a binational panel for an opinion as to whether the changes are inconsistent with the GATT or with the NAFTA's object and purpose and, specifically, whether the amendment could have the effect of overturning a prior decision by a binational panel constituted to review a final antidumping and countervailing duty determination (discussed below). The panel must issue a final declaratory opinion within 134 days of the selection of its chairperson, following which the parties have 90 days to consult and find a mutually satisfactory solution. If the panel recommends changes to the amending legislation, but corrective legislation or another mutually satisfactory solution is not enacted within nine months following the consultation period, the party requesting the panel may take comparable action or terminate the agreement (with regard to the amending party) on 60 day's notice in writing (Article 1903).

Panel Review of Final Determinations

The core of the NAFTA's dispute settlement mechanism with respect to antidumping and countervailing duties provides that each party will allow a mechanism of binational panel review to replace domestic judicial review of final determinations by the relevant agency to impose such duties (Article 1904). The purpose of the panel review is to ensure that such determinations are actually consistent with the relevant laws of the importing party. A request for a panel must be made within 30 days of the official notice of the final determination. Parties may request such review on their own initiative but must in any case do so if requested by a person who would otherwise be entitled to judicial review of the decision under the laws of the importing party. A panel's final decision must be rendered within 315 days of the date on which the panel was requested. (See Box 1 for a discussion of the procedure by which panelists are appointed.)

The panel may uphold a final determination by the investigating authorities of the importing party, or it may remand it for action not inconsistent with the panel's decision. The panel's decision will be binding on the involved parties, and parties are specifically

---

Box 1: *Selection of Panelists for Disputes on Antidumping and Countervailing Duties (Annex 1901.2)*

The parties will maintain a roster of at least 75 candidates (25 from each NAFTA country) to serve as panelists. The roster will include judges or former judges to the fullest extent practicable. The five persons forming a panel will normally be appointed from the roster. In addition, a majority of the panelists must be lawyers in good standing. Within 30 days of a request for a panel, each party involved is to appoint two panelists. (The "reverse selection" principle mandatory in panel selection under Chapter 20 does not apply to Chapter 19 panels.) The appointment must be conducted in consultation with the other party, with each party having the right to disqualify from appointment to the panel up to four candidates proposed by the other party. If a party fails to appoint a panelist within 30 days of the request for a panel or if a panelist is disqualified and no alternative panelist is selected within 45 days of the request, one will be selected by lot from the roster. If the parties are unable to agree on the selection of a fifth panelist within 55 days of the request for a panel, they will decide by lot which of them will choose the fifth panelist. The panelists must then elect a chair from among the lawyers on the panel, or appoint one by lot if there is no majority vote. A panelist active in one disputed case may not appear as counsel before another panel. Unless they violate protective orders or disclosure undertakings covering proprietary business information or other privileged information, panelists are immune from lawsuit and other legal process relating to their official capacity.

---

forbidden to provide a right of appeal from a panel's decision to its domestic courts.[5]

The Extraordinary Challenge Procedure

Panel decisions can be subjected to an extraordinary challenge if an involved party alleges

---

5 Conversely, in cases where neither party sought a panel review of an original final determination, a revised final determination issued as a direct result of a judicial review of the original determination cannot be reviewed by a NAFTA panel.

- that a member of the panel violated the rules of conduct (for example, by being guilty of bias or of a serious conflict of interest);
- that the panel seriously departed from a fundamental rule of procedure; or
- that it manifestly exceeded its powers, authority, or jurisdiction (for example, by failing to apply the appropriate standard of review);

and if that party claims that any one of the above actions has materially affected the panel's decision and threatens the integrity of the review process itself.

To decide the issue, an Extraordinary Challenge Committee, composed of three members selected from a 15-person roster comprising judges or former federally appointed judges (five from each country), will be established by the parties involved. Each party selects one member from the roster, and the two parties decide by lot which of them will select the third member from the roster. The committee must be formed within 15 days of a request for it, and has 90 days to determine whether the above-mentioned grounds for appealing the panel's decision can be established. If it finds that they can, the committee can vacate the panel's decision (in which case a new panel is established) or remand it to the panel for action not inconsistent with the committee's decision. If grounds for appeal cannot be established, the committee will deny the challenge and the original panel decision will stand.

Safeguarding the Panel System

Should 45 days of mandated consultation prove fruitless, the complaining party may request the establishment of a special committee to investigate complaints that the other party's domestic laws impede the functioning of the panel system, on the grounds that they have

- prevented the establishment of a panel requested by the complaining party;

- prevented such a panel from rendering a final decision;
- prevented the implementation of that panel's decision; or
- resulted in failure to provide opportunity for an independent review of a final determination by an investigating authority (Article 1905).

If the special committee (its roster and method of selecting committee members are the same as for extraordinary challenge committees) makes an affirmative finding on any of the above grounds and if the complaint has not been resolved to the committee's satisfaction within 60 days of the issuance of the committee's report, the complaining party may either suspend operation of the binational panel reviews with respect to the party complained against or suspend benefits accruing to that party under the terms of the NAFTA "as may be appropriate under the circumstances."

Consultations on Antidumping and Countervailing Duties

The parties agree to consult at least annually on the implementation and operation of the dispute settlement mechanism applying to antidumping and countervailing duty actions. In addition, they agree to consult on the possibility of developing more effective rules and disciplines concerning the use of government subsidies, as well as on the possibility of implementing a substitute system of rules for dealing with unfair transborder pricing practices and government subsidization (Article 1907).

Investor-State Dispute Resolution under the NAFTA

Grounds for Calling on Dispute Settlement

In addition to Chapter 20, which spells out the process for resolving investment disputes between the signatory governments, the NAFTA also provides, in Chapter 11, a mechanism to deal with disputes that arise between an investor and a NAFTA government.

An investor may submit a claim to arbitration if it has incurred loss or damage arising out of either

- a breach by another party of its obligations under the investment provisions of the NAFTA — for example, failing to provide sufficient grounds to give proper compensation in the event of expropriation; or
- regulatory or other administrative control exercised by a government-designated monopoly or state enterprise that has the effect of violating those same obligations (for example, through the discriminatory granting of licenses) (Articles 1116–1117).

The right to seek arbitration can be exercised only after six months following the events that gave rise to the claim, but within three years of the investor's (or its subsidiary's) having gained knowledge of both the breach and the consequent loss or damage.[6] The disputing parties are entreated to first try to settle such a claim through consultation or negotiation (Article 1118).

Choice of Arbitration Process

The disputing investor may submit a claim to arbitration under the authority of any one of the following:

- the 1965 International Convention on the Settlement of Investment Disputes between States and Nationals of Other States (the ICSID Convention), if the disputing party and the party of the investor are both party to the convention;
- the Additional Facility Rules of the International Centre for Settlement of Investment Disputes (ICSID), provided that ei-

---

6 Decisions by Canada regarding acquisitions subject to review under the *Investment Canada Act* are specifically excluded from the NAFTA dispute settlement provisions. There is a similar clause applying to Mexico. Decisions by any of the three countries to prohibit or restrict an investment on grounds of national security are also excluded from dispute settlement (Article 1138).

ther the disputing party or the party of the investor (but not necessarily both) is a party to the ICSID Convention; or

• the Arbitration Rules of the United Nations Commission on International Trade Law (UNCITRAL) (Article 1120).

If an investor (or the enterprise it controls) chooses to have its claim settled by a tribunal under any of these arbitration procedures, however, it automatically waives the right to settlement by an administrative tribunal or court under the law of any given NAFTA country (Article 1121).[7]

The Role of NAFTA Institutions in the Arbitration Process

Any interpretation of the NAFTA by the Free Trade Commission is binding on any tribunal established to settle investment disputes (Article 1131). This applies in particular to the commission's interpretation of the reservations and exceptions to the NAFTA's investment provisions that are set out in the annexes to the agreement (Article 1132).

Along the same lines, when investment disputes involve the financial services industry, and the disputing party argues that the disputed measure was taken for prudential purposes, the tribunal may not proceed until the NAFTA's Financial Services Committee — or, failing that, a NAFTA arbitral panel set up under the special rules that apply to the financial services sector — has ruled on the validity of the disputing party's argument. The decision of the committee or the panel in this matter is binding on the tribunal (Article 1415).

Resolution of Disputes

A tribunal may award monetary damages, with applicable interest, or restitution of property (in which case monetary damages and

---

7 Investors do retain the right to bring proceedings for injunctive, declaratory, or other extraordinary relief.

interest in lieu of restitution are also an acceptable substitute), but not punitive damages (Article 1135). If a disputing party fails to comply with a final award, the party of the investor may request that the Free Trade Commission establish an arbitral panel under the NAFTA's general dispute settlement procedure to consider whether the party failing to comply is in breach of its obligations under the NAFTA. The party of the investor may also seek enforcement of the arbitration under the ICSID or other relevant international conventions.

Disputes Involving the Financial Services Industry

Modifications to the General Dispute Settlement Mechanism

The general dispute settlement provisions set forth in Chapter 20 of the NAFTA are modified for disputes arising under the agreement's financial services chapter. The parties must jointly maintain a special roster of 15 potential financial services panelists, appointed by consensus for renewable three-year terms, who must have expertise or experience in financial services law or practice (Article 1414). A dispute settlement panel may be composed entirely of individuals qualified to serve on this roster, or it may include individuals qualified to be panelists under the general dispute settlement provisions set forth in Chapter 20. If the party complained against has stated that the disputed measure was adopted for prudential reasons, the chair of the panel must be selected from individuals qualified to be members of the special financial services roster.

Suspension of Benefits

As noted above, if a NAFTA dispute settlement panel finds that a disputed measure is inconsistent with the terms of the NAFTA, the complaining party may suspend benefits that would otherwise accrue to the offending party under the agreement. The extent of the suspension of benefits, however, is constrained in the following ways:

- If the disputed measure affects only the financial services sector, the complaining party may suspend benefits only in that sector.
- If the measure affects only other sectors, the complaining party may not suspend benefits in the financial services sector.
- If the measure affects the financial services sector and any other sector, benefits in the financial services sector can be suspended only to the point at which the suspended benefits have an effect equivalent to the effect of the measure in the complaining country's financial sector.

Financial Services Committee and Consultations

The NAFTA also establishes a Financial Services Committee. Each member country's principal representative on the committee will be an official responsible for financial services (Article 1412). In many ways, the committee will mirror, with respect to the NAFTA's financial services provisions and the specific dispute settlement procedures for that sector, the role that the Free Trade Commission plays for the agreement as a whole. Indeed, the commission can deem consultations of the Financial Services Committee to have the same effect as consultations under the NAFTA's general dispute settlement mechanism. In addition, there are special provisions for member countries to give due consideration to another member's request for consultations on financial services (Article 1413), as well as for the settlement of investment disputes involving financial services, as discussed earlier.

Other Institutions

Rules of Origin and Customs Procedures

The NAFTA establishes a Working Group on Rules of Origin, comprising representatives from each member country. The working group will be responsible for monitoring the implementation and administration by customs authorities of all customs-related aspects of Chapter 3, on national treatment and market access; Chapter 4, on the rules of origin; and Chapter 5, on customs procedures, including the Uniform Regulations (Article 513).

At the request of any member country, the working group will endeavor to agree to any proposed modification of the aforementioned NAFTA provisions. If it fails to resolve matters submitted to it by any member country (or by the working group's customs subgroup) within 30 days, any member may request that procedures be initiated under the NAFTA's general dispute settlement mechanism, starting with a meeting of the Free Trade Commission (in accordance with the procedures described earlier concerning general dispute settlement).

Sanitary and Phytosanitary Measures and Standards

When a party to the agreement notifies the Free Trade Commission of its intention to request consultations with another party regarding the application of the section of the NAFTA's agricultural chapter dealing with sanitary and phytosanitary measures, the commission may, if it does not consider the matter itself, refer the matter to a working group for nonbinding technical advice or recommendations (Article 723). In the event that these consultations fail to achieve resolution, procedures are initiated, by agreement of the parties involved, under the NAFTA's general dispute settlement mechanism. Exactly the same procedure applies to consultations on any standards-related measure (Article 914).

Publication and Notification of Law

In order to facilitate communication between, or among, the parties to the NAFTA on matters covered by the agreement, each party has agreed to designate a contact point that will be responsible to identify, and to assist in communications with, the responsible officials within their own government (Article 1801). The parties further agree to promptly publish or otherwise make available any proposed domestic laws, regulations, procedures, and administrative rulings that generally apply to any matter covered by the NAFTA, and to allow interested parties a reasonable opportunity to comment on the measures (Article 1802). Furthermore, a member country is to notify any other interested member of any proposed or actual measures that might substantially affect that member's interests under the agreement (Article 1803). Signatories to the NAFTA also undertake to provide fair administrative proceedings toward persons of another member country, including a fair review and appeal process (Articles 1804 and 1805).

How Does the NAFTA Differ from the FTA and the GATT?

Differences between the NAFTA and the FTA

General Dispute Settlement

The NAFTA introduces a number of modifications to the general dispute settlement mechanism contained in Chapter 18 (on institutional provisions) of the Canada-US Free Trade Agreement (FTA). Under the FTA, member countries could bring a matter to binding arbitration as long as there was a political consensus to do so at the level of the omission (which was called the Canada-United States Commission). Indeed, members were obligated under the FTA to refer a dispute to binding arbitration if it involved the emergency reimposition of duties by a party to the agreement. In addition, a party could request that the dispute be referred to a panel of experts, whose recommendations on how to settle the dispute the commission would normally follow.

The NAFTA eliminates the option of binding arbitration, but strengthens the role of panels, which it refers to as "arbitral panels" — rather than "panels of experts," the term used by the FTA. Under normal circumstances, the disputing parties are now to be instructed directly — rather than through the commission, as was the case under the FTA — to conform to the recommendations of the panels.

The process of selecting panelists is also somewhat different under the NAFTA. Under the FTA, the chair of a panel was normally a national of one of the disputing parties. Under the NAFTA, panelists are normally selected from the roster, which can include nationals of a NAFTA country that is *not* a party to the dispute. Furthermore, under the FTA, each side to the dispute selected panel members from among its own nationals; under the NAFTA, the principle of "reverse selection" applies, whereby each side chooses panel members from among nationals of the other side. These and other innovations — such as the explicit right of countries to request that a scientific review board assist the work of the panel on factual matters — should help strengthen the credibility of the panels.

As well, the role of the Secretariat — which, under the FTA, was set up primarily to facilitate dispute settlement in matters of anti-dumping and countervailing duty laws (Chapter 19 in both agreements) — has been expanded in the NAFTA to assist the commission in administering dispute settlements in general.

Disputes on Antidumping and Countervailing Duties

With respect to disputes involving antidumping and countervailing duties, the text of the NAFTA mirrors, for the most part, that of the FTA. However, the few existing differences are potentially important. The roster from which panelists are normally chosen must, under the NAFTA, include judges and former judges "to the fullest extent practicable," whereas "general familiarity with international trade law" was the corresponding standard under the FTA. Chapter 19 panels under both the FTA and the NAFTA are directed to apply the standards of review that a US, Canadian, or (under the NAFTA) Mexican court would apply in reviewing an antidumping or countervailing duty determination. The NAFTA, however, states explicitly that such panels will be considered to have exceeded their power, authority, or jurisdiction — and hence be subject to having their decision reversed by an Extraordinary Challenge Committee — if they fail to apply the same standards of review as would a domestic court. This link was only implicit in the FTA.

Under the NAFTA, the panel review system for disputes pertaining to antidumping and countervailing duties is clearly meant to be permanent, whereas the Chapter 19 provisions under the FTA were assured to be in effect only until the end of 1995. The deadline was written into the FTA because the two parties had agreed to develop a substitute system of rules on antidumping and countervailing duties by that time. If they had failed to do so, either party would have been free to terminate the agreement. To that end, the two countries had set up a working group that was seeking to develop a substitute system of rules for dealing with unfair pricing and government subsidization.

In contrast, the NAFTA's undertaking to consult "on the potential to develop more effective rules and disciplines concerning the use of government subsidies and on the potential for reliance on a substitute system of rules for dealing with unfair transborder pricing practices and government subsidization" establishes no deadlines and provides no special institutional framework for dealing with these key market access issues.[8]

Investor-State Disputes

The FTA provided that investment disputes could be settled under the terms of the agreement's general dispute settlement procedure, with two modifications: attempts were to be made to select panelists who were experienced and competent in the field of international investment, and the panels were to take into consideration internationally recognized rules for commercial arbitration in their handling of investment disputes. The NAFTA clearly makes this last

---

8 The issue of a substitute regime for antidumping and countervailing duties between Canada and the United States is often referred to as the "unfinished business" of the FTA and the NAFTA.

point the centerpiece of its mechanism for settling investment disputes, by explicitly allowing parties to a dispute to request international arbitration. The panel system outlined in Chapter 20 remains
a forum for the settlement of government-to-government disputes
involving investment issues, as well as an ultimate appeal mechanism in cases of failure to comply with international arbitration. In
addition, any international tribunal dealing with an investment
dispute under the terms of the NAFTA must ultimately rely on the
Free Trade Commission's interpretation of the NAFTA provisions.

Disputes Involving the Financial Services Industry

Under the NAFTA, disputes involving financial services will be
referred to the general dispute settlement mechanism, with a modified roster of panelists to reflect financial industry expertise and with
a mechanism to insulate the fallout from disputes in other sectors on
the financial services sector, and vice versa. Under the FTA, only
disputes within the insurance industry could be dealt with through
the general dispute settlement mechanism. Other matters involving
the financial services sector were handled by consultations between
the Canadian Department of Finance and the US Department of the
Treasury.

Differences between the NAFTA and the GATT

Because the NAFTA's dispute settlement mechanisms were broadly
inspired by those of the FTA, the key differences between the
NAFTA's and the existing GATT's dispute resolution mechanisms
can be described as essentially the same as those between the FTA
and the GATT. In particular, the NAFTA, unlike the GATT, imposes
severe time constraints on solving disputes; moreover, dispute settlement is normally binding on the NAFTA signatories, which it is not,

at the moment, on the GATT signatories, since the latter are able to block the adoption of panel reports at the GATT Council.

The latest GATT negotiations, however, have succeeded in streamlining that agreement's dispute settlement mechanism and making the recommendations of its panels more enforceable. Hence, when the new GATT provisions are implemented in 1995, the relative advantage of the NAFTA's mechanisms will be diminished. Furthermore, as already noted, the NAFTA restricts its signatories' freedom to use the GATT dispute settlement process, notably when the disputes involve environmental standards.

The Significance of the Provisions

The mechanism for general dispute settlement seems to have been strengthened in the NAFTA relative to what it was in the FTA. In particular, the Secretariat has a more prominent role in overall dispute settlement, and the new selection process for panelists is likely to enhance the functioning and authority of the arbitral panels. These features should offset the nominal elimination of binding arbitration as a way of settling disputes, a route that was in any event subject to political agreement among the parties under the FTA.

In certain specific instances, particularly in connection with disputes involving standards, the NAFTA shows a somewhat greater preference than did the FTA for using North American dispute settlement mechanisms over those of the GATT. In such circumstances, Canada may be obliged to have recourse to the NAFTA dispute settlement process if it is a complaining party. (The NAFTA dispute settlement mechanism has been strengthened with respect to standards-related matters by the introduction of scientific review boards as a resource for arbitral panels.)

The dispute settlement mechanism as it pertains to antidumping and countervailing duties also seems to be somewhat more restrictive under the NAFTA than it was under the FTA. In both cases, the binational panels substitute for domestic judicial review, to the extent that they must rely on the same standards of review.

However, the specification that the panels must be composed as far as possible of judges and former judges may have had the serious effect, in practical terms, of excluding nonlegal experts, who might be more likely to hold the administrative agencies that are responsible for imposing antidumping or countervailing duties to high standards of proof when they are determining, for example, whether an industry has been injured by imports. Judges may tend to defer more to the interpretations of the administrative agencies in these matters.[9] A similar direction seems evident in the provision that "failing to apply the appropriate standards of review" will be an explicit ground for appealing panel decisions through an Extraordinary Challenge Committee.

The NAFTA has dropped the FTA requirement for a working group to develop a substitute system of rules for dealing with unfair pricing and government subsidization. The development of new rules would have represented a major step toward Canada's goal of total exemption from US antidumping and countervailing actions. It is true that the working group established under the FTA did not, in fact, arrive at a workable substitute system, and the chances that it would have done so within its seven-year mandate were slim. Nonetheless, the NAFTA's weak language concerning "consultations" on "the potential" for a substitute system of rules, with no time frame attached to it, is surely a major disappointment relative to what was contained in the FTA.[10] In any event, as a condition for implementing the NAFTA, the new Canadian Liberal government elected in October 1993 was able to wrest from the United States and

---

9 To defer to the administrative agencies' judgment has certainly been the tendency of domestic judicial reviews. See Thomas M. Boddez and Michael J. Trebilcock, *Unfinished Business: Reforming Trade Remedy Laws in North America*, Policy Study 17 (Toronto: C.D. Howe Institute, 1993). While Canada has placed only one judge on its roster of 25 candidates for Chapter 19 panels, the number of nonlawyers on the NAFTA roster has shrunk dramatically relative to the FTA roster.

10 It is true, however, that the FTA also fell short, in that it did not explicitly provide for the continuation of the dispute settlement procedure (in matters of antidumping and countervailing duties) in the event that negotiations for a substitute system of rules failed — an omission that had raised questions as to whether the panel system would have been continued beyond 1995.

Mexico a promise to set up working groups that will seek trilateral codes on dumping and subsidies by the end of 1995, in the spirit — if not the letter — of the original FTA.

The automatic appeal to international arbitration in the case of investor-state disputes (at the investor's option) in no way limits Canada's options of accepting or rejecting large foreign investments. Since neither Canada nor Mexico are currently signatories to the ICSID Convention, the agreement means, for now, that investor-state disputes involving NAFTA parties will follow the UNCITRAL Arbitration Rules. Thus, in the event of an investor-state dispute under the terms of the NAFTA, any NAFTA country, including Canada, may have to justify before an international tribunal the conditions under which it chooses to expropriate foreign investors and the tribunal's decision will be binding.

An all-encompassing trading relationship such as that between Canada and the United States (or between the United States and Mexico) is bound to cause a wide variety of technical issues to arise, and it is important to try to solve them at the bureaucratic or diplomatic level before they become ensnared in the political process. The NAFTA's better developed consultative mechanisms and various advisory and working groups will significantly enhance the signatories' ability to defuse disputes at an early stage.

Concerns about the Provisions

Studies show that the dispute settlement process under the FTA was a gain for Canada relative to the status quo,[11] but legitimate questions have been raised as to whether these gains were preserved in their entirety in the NAFTA. Three major concerns emerge. First, are the NAFTA's dispute settlement mechanisms weaker than the FTA's from the point of view of trade liberalization? Second, has Canada

---

11 After studying various cases that came before the FTA's Chapter 19 panels, Boddez and Trebilcock (*Unfinished Business*) conclude that, in a number of those cases, the review of US administrative agencies' decisions by the panels came out in favor of Canadian exporters.

abandoned its commitment to negotiate completely open access to the US market, entirely free of harassment under US trade remedy laws? Third, has Canada constrained its rights under the GATT?

As we have seen, the NAFTA's general dispute settlement mechanism seems in many respects to be stronger than that of the FTA, and has been supplemented by a sharper focus on dispute avoidance mechanisms. The panel review system for antidumping and countervailing duties has been given a nudge toward interpreting the determinations of administrative agencies in the same way that a domestic judicial review process would, but the important gains inherent in the very existence of such a review system are, on the whole, maintained.

Although the NAFTA still makes reference to Canada's objective of negotiating a system of rules that would lead to fewer or, ideally, no antidumping and countervailing actions between the two countries whatsoever, the commitment has been weakened somewhat, and the issue will possibly have to be addressed on an industry-by-industry basis. Not only has the language on the subject weaker in the NAFTA than it was in the FTA, but, now that Mexico is to be included in all further consultations on the subject, the United States' strong political incentive to retain antidumping regulations against that country may further delay a resolution. Once again, however, the trilateral negotiations to which Canada, the United States, and Mexico agreed in December 1993 will mitigate this drawback of the NAFTA.

The NAFTA provides that a country whose domestic environmental standards are challenged by a trading partner on the grounds that they are harmful to the latter's trade may request that the dispute be resolved via NAFTA mechanisms rather than at the GATT. This provision deprives Canada of some of the flexibility it formerly had in challenging US environmental standards that might hurt Canadian exports. Under the terms of the NAFTA, before the country disputing the standard can seek any kind of redress, it must in essence show that the standard is an unnecessary barrier to trade. By contrast, at the GATT, the simple fact that a new standard had the effect of reducing trade could, under certain circumstances, entitle the complainant to some redress. Whatever the merits of including environmental safeguards in trade agreements, it is the smaller markets within the free trade area that is potentially most vulnerable to trade-restricting standards adopted by the larger economy, rather than vice versa. Limiting the smaller countries' right to obtain compensation for such measures leaves them more vulnerable than before.

Overall, the NAFTA's dispute settlement provisions preserve most of the gains achieved under the FTA. In some areas, the NAFTA improves on the FTA in ways that should make the resolution of disputes between the trading partners smoother. In other ways, however, it seems to make it somewhat more difficult for dispute settlement panels to reverse trade-restricting measures than was the case under the FTA and the GATT. With respect to dumping and subsidies disputes, which are Canada's most important remaining trade concern, the NAFTA does not constitute a step forward.

Part III

The NAFTA's Impact on Canada

Chapter 9

Did Canada Achieve
Its Negotiating Objectives?

What Were the
Negotiating Objectives?

In negotiating the NAFTA, each country had a specific set of objectives. Mexico, like Canada earlier, was seeking better access to the US market not only for the standard economic benefits that increased trade would offer, but also to ensure that its existing trade would not suffer from renewed US protectionist measures. Mexico also wished to use this free trade policy to complement and strengthen its domestic market-oriented reforms. For its part, the United States was not only pursuing the broad vision of a free trade area extending from the Yukon to the Yucatan set out in President Bush's Enterprise of the Americas initiative, with the large gains in income such openness promised throughout the hemisphere; it was also seeking to address areas of conflict in US-Mexican trade and investment through the NAFTA negotiations. In addition, the United States required assurance that the NAFTA would not transform Mexico — or, indeed, other future less-developed participants in hemispheric free trade — into platforms for Japanese and other transplant producers seeking duty-free access to the US market.

Once the United States and Mexico decided to liberalize their trade, maintaining the status quo ceased to be a viable option for Canada. If it participated in the negotiations, Canada could

- acquire the benefits of free trade with Mexico, in terms of access not only for Canadian products and services to the Mexican market but also for low-cost Mexican products to Canadian industry and consumers;

- reduce irritants in its trade with the United States through the forum of these negotiations; and
- defend its interests by, among other objectives, ensuring that Mexico's maquiladora system would be appropriately reformed, that it would acquire any special benefits that Mexico might be able to negotiate in terms of access to the US market, and that the benefits of the Canada-US Free Trade Agreement (FTA) would be protected.

Had Canada chosen not to participate, it would have had to face the locational and other disadvantages of being an outsider to a Mexican-US free trade arrangement. Moreover, it would have allowed future hemispheric trade liberalization to evolve in an unfavorable direction, creating a "hub-and-spoke" pattern, with each of the smaller countries maintaining separate bilateral agreements with the United States.

The reasons compelling Canada to participate in the NAFTA are probably much the same as those that would compel it to participate in the Uruguay Round of negotiations under the General Agreement on Tariffs and Trade (GATT) or any other initiative toward multilateral liberalization taken by its trading partners — for example, by members of the Organisation for Economic Co-operation and Development. Indeed, when a country's major trading partners are moving toward liberalizing their trade, not only is it beneficial to be included, but it can be very costly to be left out.[1]

Officially, Canada's objectives in the talks were as follows:[2]

---

1 It would not be imperative for Canada to participate in a liberalization of trade between, say, Australia and New Zealand, because few of its markets and supply sources are located there. Because Australia and New Zealand are not major trading partners for Canada, it would have little to lose by being excluded and little to gain from participating.

2 As set out in a speech delivered on August 12, 1992, by Michael Wilson, Canada's minister for international trade, and in an August 1992 Canadian government press release entitled "North American Free Trade: An Overview and Description," p. iv. The objectives were outlined in similar terms in a December 1991 Situation Report issued by the Office of North American Free Trade Negotiations, External Affairs and International Trade Canada.

- to gain access for Canadian goods, services, and capital to Mexico — one of the fastest growing and most promising economies in the world — on an equal footing with the United States;
- to resolve a number of specific irritants with the United States that occurred within the context of the more intense trade and investment relationship of the past few years, and to ensure no reduction in the benefits and obligations of the FTA; and
- to ensure that Canada remained an attractive location for investors wishing to serve the whole North American market.

It is instructive that all three of Canada's stated objectives relate to its trading relationship with the United States, whereas only two make reference to Mexico. This is an appropriate reflection of the fact that trade with the United States is of far greater importance for Canada than trade with Mexico or any other country.

By and large, Canada achieved its stated objectives, and in some cases even exceeded them. In certain other respects, however, the result of Canada's negotiating efforts fell short of its targets.

Access to the Mexican Market

The verdict on the objective of gaining access to the Mexican market is fairly unambiguous: the NAFTA will result in a substantial opening up of that market to Canadian products and services. With a few exceptions — notably, where Canada resisted liberalizing its trade with Mexico in certain agricultural products — Canadian exports will enter Mexico on the same terms as US exports, and those terms are far more favorable than in the past. As detailed in preceding chapters, Mexico will, over time, remove tariffs and a range of nontariff barriers — such as import licensing requirements, restrictions on foreign providers of financial services, and its Auto Decree — that created obstacles for Canadian exports in the past. Canadian firms will also be able to bid on a significant share of the Mexican government's procurement contracts on a par with Mexican and US firms.

Access will not be completely free, however, since Mexico still restricts some of its trade and Mexican trade remedies remain in place (as do US and Canadian trade remedies). The NAFTA will, however, constrain the use of trade remedies; moreover, Mexico is committed to revising its trade remedy laws.

Resolving Irritants and Protecting FTA Benefits

Irritants in Canada-US Trade Relations

A number of NAFTA provisions will have a positive effect on some existing and potential bilateral trade irritants. However, the precise practical effect of these changes on actual disputes remains to be seen. By making the rules of origin more transparent and less subject to arbitrary rulings by customs officials, the NAFTA promises to minimize the occurrence of disputes such as the one over the 1992 Honda Civic ruling. However, as we have already seen, this gain came at the cost of making the rules of origin more stringent for certain industries, including automobiles.

The NAFTA obligates the signatories to ensure that the energy regulatory bodies within their territories will, "to the maximum extent practicable," avoid disruption of contractual relationships. This position is expected to help natural gas producers in Alberta in their attempt to prevent the California Public Utilities Commission from unilaterally modifying its long-term contracts with Canadian energy producers. Such "help" will come only in the form of moral suasion, however, since the agreement does not provide an enforceable discipline against subfederal entities.[3]

---

3 See André Plourde, *Energy and the NAFTA*, C.D. Howe Institute Commentary 45 (Toronto: C.D. Howe Institute, March 1993).

Another example of the NAFTA's probable beneficial impact on bilateral disputes is in the area of standards, where increased discipline may help to prevent such restraints on trade as the 1989 US action against imports of Canadian lobsters because of their size.

The NAFTA's permanent inclusion of the FTA dispute settlement mechanism for disputes over antidumping and countervailing duties can be seen as a benefit to Canada. Under Chapter 19 of the FTA, this mechanism ensured, as far as possible, the fair resolution of such disputes; in practice, it facilitated the reversal of a number of spurious charges of dumping or subsidization against Canadian exporters by importers in the US market.[4] It must be recognized, however, that the reason such mechanisms need to exist under the NAFTA at all is that the parties to the agreement retain the full use of their antidumping and countervailing duty laws against one another. Clearly, Canada's most important objective in this area is to negotiate a substitute system that would prevent such disputes from occurring in the first place. As explained in the preceding chapter, the NAFTA did fall short with respect to this more difficult but also much more important objective. The December 1993 parallel accord between Canada, the United States, and Mexico to negotiate a dumping and subsidies code is expected to go at least some distance toward correcting that situation.

Keeping the Benefits of the FTA Intact

Has the NAFTA cemented Canada's gains from the FTA? The short answer is "by and large, yes."

One Canadian benefit from the FTA that could not be saved by Canadian participation in the NAFTA was Canada's preference over Mexico in the US market. This benefit was lost the moment free trade was implemented between Mexico and the United States. Of course, Canada and Mexico together now share preference in the US market over all other countries.

---

4 Thomas M. Boddez and Michael J. Trebilcock, *Unfinished Business: Reforming Trade Remedy Laws in North America*, Policy Study 17 (Toronto: C.D. Howe Institute, 1993).

Although it was impossible for Canada's negotiators to prevent the loss of this Canadian benefit from the FTA, they were successful in ensuring against an even more damaging possibility: that Mexico would get *better* treatment than Canada in the US market. (This was a possibility in areas other than tariffs, which had been eliminated under the FTA.) Had Canada not participated in the NAFTA, it might well have encountered this result in the area of government procurement, where the United States provided better access in the NAFTA than Canada had achieved under the FTA. By participating in the NAFTA, however, Canada now benefits from the same favorable treatment as Mexico.

Canada preserved not only the liberalization of trade with the United States that was gained under the FTA, but also the *exemptions* from it — notably of cultural industries and agricultural marketing boards (although the NAFTA will not protect the latter from changes stemming from the new GATT agreement). There is still the question of whether protecting these sectors is in Canada's best interest; however, the NAFTA did allay the fears of critics who were concerned that exemptions secured under the FTA would be put back on the table and either compromised or eliminated. It also allayed fears that existing Canadian safeguards in the automotive sector, introduced as part of the 1965 auto pact might be eliminated. Indeed, one of the most difficult tasks facing the Canadian negotiators may have been protecting those safeguards at the same time that Mexico was having to eliminate its Auto Decree.

There are a number of areas in which the NAFTA has introduced improvements on the FTA for Canada:

- Not only has the NAFTA given Canada better access to the US government procurement market than the FTA had provided, it has also extended the deadline for eliminating duty drawbacks from 1994 (the deadline under the FTA) to 1996.
- It has provided clearer rules of origin as well as some relief for Canadian exporters who are unable to satisfy the NAFTA rules of origin and are therefore still paying a US or Mexican tariff.

- It has introduced downward harmonization of tariffs in the computer industry — a measure that offers a model for avoiding, in future hemispheric negotiations, the rules-of-origin problems that arose in the NAFTA in other sectors.
- It has liberalized cross-border land transportation, which will provide benefits for Canada-US trade that were not available under the FTA (although cabotage is not liberalized under the deal, Canadian trucking companies should now find shipping into the United States more profitable).

Ensuring that Canada Remains an Attractive Investment Location

The creation of a regional free trade area is expected to make North America more attractive as an investment location. By participating in the NAFTA, Canada — like the United States and Mexico — becomes a location from which overseas investors can service the entire North American market. In addition, the NAFTA provisions on investment and intellectual property rights are likely to strengthen foreign investors' confidence in the entire free trade area. The more complex question is: How will Canada fare as a location in competition with its NAFTA partners?

By participating in the NAFTA, Canada has avoided a major locational disadvantage in competing with the United States. Had Canada opted out, the United States would have become a trading hub with two "spokes" — that is two bilateral agreements, one with Canada and one with Mexico — and perhaps, with more to come later, in the form of bilateral agreements with various other countries in the hemisphere. Under such an arrangement, a firm locating in the United States would acquire duty-free access to the markets of all participating countries in the hemisphere; if it were to locate in Canada, it would have access only to the US market. The choice for investors would be clear.

Despite having avoided this major investment disadvantage, however, Canada still faces challenges in maintaining its attractiveness as an investment location. For example, although the NAFTA provisions on investment and intellectual property rights apply to all three countries, their greatest perceived effect may be in reducing the risk of investing in Mexico, making that location appealing enough to attract some investment away from both Canada and the United States.

Investors reviewing the location of planned or existing facilities must also consider the impact of any remaining nontariff measures. If producers in one country find that, despite the existence of a trade agreement, access to a partner country is still impeded — because of stringent rules of origin, the threat of antidumping duties, or protectionist standards, for example — they may decide to locate production facilities in the larger market of the two in order to minimize the potentially costly rules, constraints, or harassment they have to face.[5] Such decisions by investors would obviously cause a serious reduction in the benefits that smaller countries — Canada and Mexico, in the case of the NAFTA — would normally expect to obtain from membership in a free trade area. Because Canada still does not have unimpeded access to the US market, the NAFTA still leaves Canada facing obstacles in its attempt to attract North American investment.

However, not participating in the NAFTA would have left Canada in an even worse situation, since it would have had to face these same difficulties — and more; specifically, firms locating in

---

5 Within any free trade area, restrictive rules of origin not only protect all members against outsiders, as traditionally recognized, but also benefit the country with the largest market as opposed to its smaller partners. To illustrate this less obvious effect, note that a Japanese firm wishing to sell in the large US market needs simply to locate there to avoid having to satisfy any rule of origin (since it will not be selling its product across any border within the NAFTA). In contrast, if it locates instead in Canada or Mexico, it must satisfy rules of origin in order to sell duty free across the border into the United States. The more stringent the rules of origin, the greater becomes the incentive to locate in the United States, the larger market. Thus, the more demanding rules of origin in the NAFTA for certain sectors protect the United States from its "free" trade partners (see Ronald J. Wonnacott, *The NAFTA: Fortress North America?* C.D. Howe Institute Commentary 54 [Toronto: C.D. Howe Institute, November 1993]). This obvious disadvantage for Canada must be weighed against the fact that the NAFTA rules of origin are now clearer and, in some cases, more flexible, and generally less likely to create disputes between the trading partners.

Canada would not have had the same free access to Mexican markets and duty-free inputs as firms locating in the United States. Consequently, Canada would have left itself at a permanent disadvantage in competing with the United States for foreign direct investment.

Making Canada a More Competitive Economy

The liberalization of trade between Canada and Mexico has provided Canada with a benefit that was not explicitly stated in its official set of objectives — namely, that Canadian barriers against imports from Mexico have also been eliminated.[6] This is arguably not as important a benefit for Canada as the elimination of Mexican barriers against Canadian exports, as can be seen most clearly in the case of the automobile industry. Most automotive equipment — Canada's largest import from Mexico by a large margin[7] — has entered Canada duty free since 1965 in accordance with the auto pact provisions that safeguard Canadian assembly (but that have also, in this case, paradoxically provided an incentive for Mexican parts to be imported into Canada). In this area, then, Canadian tariff elimination under the NAFTA is likely to mean little cost savings on imports. By contrast, the NAFTA's elimination of the Mexican Auto Decree, which had essentially blocked Canadian exports, will offer a much greater potential benefit to Canada.

Nonetheless, the benefits to Canada of removing barriers to imports may still be substantial. Not only will less expensive Mexican

---

6 The stated objectives of politicians in any trade negotiation tend to follow the formula "reduce foreign barriers, hang on to our own." For example, the terms of success for Canada in the agricultural negotiations were described as the ability to "expand market opportunities for [Canadian exports of] red meat and grains, while fully retaining our existing system of national supply management for the dairy, poultry and eggs sectors" (Government of Canada, *North American Free Trade Agreement*, p. ix).

7 In 1992, Canada imported just under $1.6 billion in automotive equipment from Mexico, while imports of all other types of machinery and equipment amounted to less than $0.7 billion and all other imports from Mexico to just over $0.5 billion.

goods — and competitively priced Canadian products — directly benefit Canadian consumers, but liberalized imports will inject a greater degree of international competition into Canadian markets, resulting in a more efficient and more competitive Canadian economy. The ability of Canadian firms to purchase duty-free inputs from Mexico will make them better able to compete in world markets, particularly against US industries in Canada, the United States, and elsewhere.[8] Obtaining this benefit is critical, since competing US firms will be getting it as well, and it is competition with US firms in the Canadian and, particularly, the US marketplace that represents the greatest challenge to Canadian producers. Paradoxically, trade liberalization with Mexico may well have its most significant effect on Canadian industry in improving its ability to compete not in Mexico or even Canada, but in the United States. This is where Canada's major competitive challenge lies, and its ability to compete there will be enhanced by access to inexpensive Mexican inputs.

---

8 In the absence of a perfect redistributive mechanism, there are both winners and losers from any change, whether it be a shift in demand or a technological advance, that directly or indirectly changes price. The same is true of a trade agreement such as the NAFTA because it will lower the Canadian domestic price of imports and import-competing products. Thus, an industry's view of the NAFTA will depend on its answer to the question: Are we using or are we competing against low-priced imports from Mexico? — and for some industries, the answer will be "both." However, the benefits to Canadian consumers and using industries are expected to exceed the loss to competing Canadian producers and the Canadian treasury — which will lose duty revenues. The likely resulting net long-term benefits will be reduced by short-run adjustment costs in competing Canadian industries, but will be augmented by other benefits not included in the traditional calculus, such as the increased competitiveness of the Canadian economy.

Chapter 10

The Impact of the NAFTA on Canada's Economy

From a Canadian standpoint, as we have seen, much of the NAFTA is concerned with preserving access to the United States market for Canadian producers on terms as good as or better than those of the existing Canada-US Free Trade Agreement (FTA), and on terms as good as those that Mexico will enjoy. In return, in the NAFTA negotiations Canada agreed to accept new constraints in trade-related areas and to open its markets to Mexican-based producers.

In its strategic implications, if not all of its details, the deal is often seen by both proponents and opponents of the NAFTA as the logical extension of the FTA. It is therefore not surprising that the nature of the criticisms and praise that surrounded the NAFTA mirrored the debate that took place in Canada over the FTA. Because of the similarities in the issues surrounding the two agreements, Canadians inevitably will assess the economic impact of the NAFTA partly on the basis of their assessment of the FTA's benefits and costs. This chapter begins by reviewing what we know about the impact of the existing FTA; it then adds Mexico to the equation.

The Lessons of the FTA

Well before the Canada-US FTA was signed in late 1987, its critics were arguing that, if the tariff wall that protected production in Canada were to be removed, lower taxes and lower labor costs in the United States — resulting from a weaker social safety net, low rates of unionization, and, in some states, "right to work" legislation —

would drive manufacturing firms established in Canada south of the border. As a result, free trade would either force Canadian workers to accept lower wages in order to save their jobs or so gut Canada's manufacturing sector that the country would have to rely even more heavily on exports of natural resources to sustain its standard of living, thereby entrenching its role as the "hewer of wood and drawer of water" for the United States and thwarting future economic development.[1]

Opponents viewed Canada's automotive sector as particularly vulnerable under the free trade scenario, as zero tariffs between Canada and the United States would remove the incentive for auto pact companies to continue to produce in Canada. (In fact, zero tariffs with the United States reduced, but did not remove, this incentive, since a duty-remission incentive remained on imports from third countries.) Opponents also characterized the United States as a fading economic star, suggesting that Canada was making the wrong choice by opening up trade links with the United States as opposed to, say, making a greater effort to penetrate the faster-growing Asian market. Many of the same arguments were brought forward in the debate over whether Canada should join the NAFTA.

Proponents, for their part, acknowledged that the Canadian economy would have to undergo significant changes under free trade — most notably, in the form of employment losses in the industries in which Canada was not internationally competitive. They argued, however, that these difficulties would be more than offset by the benefits of free trade for Canada: lower costs and greater competitiveness through specialization and expansion in areas of comparative advantage; economies of scale through longer produc-

---

1 In the words of Shirley Carr, then-president of the Canadian Labour Congress, "The government seems ready to create minimum-wage jobs while intentionally forgetting the standard of living we now enjoy, which was created by higher-paying industrial manufacturing, service, transportation, and research jobs." Cited in Laurier LaPierre, ed., *If You Love This Country: Facts and Feelings on Free Trade* (Toronto: McClelland and Stewart, 1987), p. 88.

tion runs based on improved access to the huge US market; and the dynamic impact of an open trading environment on Canadian firms' willingness to innovate and deliver the best value to their customers. Overall, employment growth would occur in industries with a higher value added than that of the industries shedding jobs, and, over the medium term, the jobs lost would be replaced by an equal or larger number of better-paying jobs.[2]

With bilateral free trade now well into its sixth year, what can we say about the realization of the pessimistic and the optimistic scenarios put forward in the original debate?

Analysts who have attempted to reach conclusions on the impact of the FTA since its implementation have focused on three dimensions: the causes of Canada's current macroeconomic conditions; microeconomic factors in manufacturing industries, such as productivity, wages, and tariff changes; and trade flows. Those who have viewed the situation from the first (macroeconomic) angle have concluded that the decline in Canada's cost competitiveness (including faster wage increases in Canada than in the United States) and cyclical factors in both countries were overwhelmingly responsible for the jobs lost in manufacturing during the 1989–91 recession. Contributing to this macroeconomic pressure was a strongly disinflationary monetary policy that raised interest rates. Throughout the 1989–91 period, the resulting rise in the value of the Canadian dollar put a heavy burden on producers of tradable goods and services. At the same time, analysts have acknowledged that employment losses since 1989 have been caused not just by macroeconomic pressures but also by a number of structural factors, of which free trade with

---

2 See, for example, Ronald J. Wonnacott and Paul Wonnacott, *Free Trade between the United States and Canada: The Potential Economic Effects* (Cambridge, Mass.: Harvard University Press, 1967); Richard G. Harris and David Cox, *Trade, Industrial Policy, and Canadian Manufacturing*, Ontario Economic Council Research Study 31 (Toronto: Ontario Economic Council, 1983); and Economic Council of Canada, *Venturing Forth: An Assessment of the Canada-US Trade Agreement* (Ottawa: Supply and Services Canada, 1988).

the United States has been one.[3] To keep this in perspective, however, preliminary results from studies that attempt to identify microeconomic pressures on industries affected by the FTA suggest that no more than one in six manufacturing jobs lost between 1989 and 1991 can be attributed to the agreement.[4]

Another way of looking at free trade that yields useful conclusions is a careful examination of the changes in trade flows between Canada and the United States, on the one hand, and Canada and its other trading partners, on the other, since the implementation of the FTA.[5] These data show that, in fact, Canada's exports to the United States over the FTA's first three years of operation were strongest in those sectors that were liberalized by the agreement (see Table 4). A particularly positive effect was evident in such nonresource-based manufacturing sectors as office, telecommunications, and precision equipment, whose exports to the United States increased by a whopping 85 percent between 1988 and 1992. In contrast, Canadian exports of the same goods to other countries languished, despite the

---

3 See Rodrigue Tremblay, "L'Émergence d'un bloc économique et commercial nord-américain: la compétitivité de l'économie canadienne et la politique du taux de change" (Université de Montréal, cahier 9212, 1992); Ontario, Treasurer of Ontario, *Renewing Ontario: A Plan for the Economy* (Toronto: Ministry of Treasury and Economics, 1992), p. 8; and Royal Bank of Canada, "Economic Restructuring in Canada," *EconoViews* (August 1993). Note that free trade is not directly blamed for *net* job losses in these studies, but is cited as one of the structural changes that have affected the economy during the period under consideration. Indeed, these authors do not exclude the possibility that free trade actually helped maintain jobs that would otherwise have been lost. In fact, Peter Pauly concluded that the FTA had a positive impact ("Macroeconomic Effects of the Canada-US Free Trade Agreement," Studies on the Economic Future of North America series [Vancouver; Toronto: Fraser Institute and University of Toronto Centre for International Studies, 1991]).

4 Noel Gaston and Daniel Trefler, "The Labour Market Consequences of the Canada-US Free Trade Agreement: A Preliminary Assessment" (University of Toronto, October 1992, mimeographed), as cited and interpreted by Leonard Waverman in "The NAFTA Agreement: A Canadian Perspective," in Steven Globerman and Michael Walker, eds., *Assessing NAFTA: A Trinational Analysis* (Vancouver: Fraser Institute, 1993).

5 See Daniel Schwanen, *A Growing Success: Canada's Trade Performance under Free Trade*, C.D. Howe Institute Commentary 52 (Toronto: C.D. Howe Institute, September 1993).

Table 4: *Trade Patterns, 1988–92*

Category of Goods	Trade 1992 (C$ billions)	% change 1988–92
Export categories liberalized by free trade: Canada's exports to the United States	49.5	33.4
Export categories liberalized by free trade: Canada's exports to the rest of the world	22.2	1.9
Export categories *not* liberalized by free trade: Canada's exports to the United States	26.1	9.0
Import categories liberalized by free trade: Canada's imports from the United States	55.6	28.4
Import categories liberalized by free trade: Canada's imports from the rest of the world	32.6	10.1
Import categories *not* liberalized by free trade: Canada's imports from the United States	15.6	0.7

Source: Daniel Schwanen, *A Growing Success: Canada's Performance under Free Trade*, C.D. Howe Institute Commentary 52 (Toronto: C.D. Howe Institute, September 1993); and Leonard Waverman, "The NAFTA Agreement: A Canadian Perspective," in Steven Gloverman and Michael Walker, eds., *Assessing NAFTA: A Trinational Analysis* (Vancouver: Fraser Institute, 1993). Imports and exports in this table exclude autos and crude oil, although Canada's exports to and trade balance with the United States in these sectors also increased over the life of the FTA.

fact that these other markets experienced stronger growth than did the United States during the same period. Even within resource-based manufacturing sectors, products for which exports to the United States most significantly outperformed exports to other countries over the life of the agreement included higher-value-added areas such as specialty papers and petrochemicals, which previously faced high tariffs into the US market. Similar calculations show that exports of services liberalized by the FTA also grew at a remarkably fast pace.

Imports from the United States rose faster in the sectors that were liberalized under free trade as well. This has been particularly true for the more traditional industries, such as furniture and clothing, as well as for such products as food-processing machines and other household goods and electrical appliances. The surge of imports in these sectors does suggest that jobs have been lost to free trade, a trend that had by and large been predicted by both supporters and opponents of the FTA. (It should be noted, however, that some portion of the increase in these imports does not reflect a Canadian job loss since it is simply trade diversion — that is, a switch by Canadian purchasers from overseas products to US products as a result of lower Canadian tariffs on US goods.) By contrast, the trade data do not confirm the validity of critics' concerns that the FTA would have a long-term negative impact on Canada's auto sector.

In many respects, these findings belie the warnings of opponents of the deal that the FTA would make Canada more dependent on exports of natural resources and hurt its automotive sector, or that free trade with a relatively slow-growth economy like that of the United States would reduce Canada's potential for growth. Rather, they show that, if anything, free trade has benefited Canada's higher-value-added industries, which are key to higher standards of living in the future, although it has done so at the expense of certain more traditional occupations (weekly wages in a typical industry experiencing growth under free trade are 20 percent higher than those in industries hurt by the FTA).[6]

By themselves, these findings do not yet show conclusively that free trade has succeeded, particularly because the jobs lost in the labor-intensive, import-competing industries probably may not have yet been replaced by an equal or higher number of jobs gained in export-expanding industries. The findings do, however, show that the agreement's detractors were too pessimistic. The objective of free trade, like technological change, is not primarily to increase employment, but to increase productivity — that is, in many cases, to reduce the labor required to produce goods. While this means that increased exports do not necessarily translate in an automatic way into more jobs, it does make the economy better able to create high-productivity, high-income jobs. The evidence so far is consistent with the view

---

6 Based on Statistics Canada data on weekly wages by industry, and Daniel Schwanen's calculation of an average wage for eight import-affected industries and eight export-expanding industries.

that the FTA is meeting that objective. Whatever positive effect it may end up having on total employment would be in addition to its expected favorable effect on productivity and incomes.

Estimates of the Economic Impact of the NAFTA

The Impact on the Overall Economy

Projections by economic models of the NAFTA's likely impact on the Canadian economy tend to be positive, but modest — something in the order of one-tenth of 1 percent of gross domestic product, or C$700 million.[7] These results are hardly surprising, since trade between Canada and Mexico is small and already relatively unimpeded by tariffs. Economic models of trade liberalization are best suited to measuring the efficiency of resource use; in those terms, not much more can be gained from the further liberalization of trade between Canada and Mexico — particularly in the way of advantages for importers in the form of cheaper imports from Mexico, since Canadian tariffs are already quite low, on average.

Once again, such results do not support the critics' dire predictions that the NAFTA would trigger an exodus of jobs from Canada. This is not to say that trade and competition with Mexico will not have a negative impact on some Canadian industries and workers, but that impact would have occurred eventually whether Canada had joined the NAFTA or not: Mexico's competitiveness would grow through free trade with the United States, and its exports to Canada would consequently increase. Some firms moved their Canadian operations to Mexico well before the NAFTA was a consideration, and some are likely to do so now that it has been implemented. As noted earlier, many Mexican imports were already entering Canada

---

7 See William G. Watson, *The Economic Impact of the NAFTA*, C.D. Howe Institute Commentary 50 (Toronto: C.D. Howe Institute, June 1993).

at low or zero rates of duty (notably autos and parts, as a direct result of the auto pact). The reason Canada was not being flooded by Mexican imports in spite of the low Canadian barriers is simple: with the exception of a few sectors, Mexican industry is not sufficiently competitive to penetrate the Canadian market on a significant scale. Despite Mexico's low wages, Canada is obviously well ahead in many facets of productivity and competitiveness.[8]

Mexico's imposition of substantial barriers against Canadian goods and services is one of the reasons that Canada has not been exporting heavily to that country. With the NAFTA, some of the more significant Mexican barriers will fall, allowing Canadian firms to export more goods and services to the Mexican market. In fact, because Mexican access to the Canadian market has been relatively open in the past, while Mexico's market remained relatively protected, there is "every likelihood that, as a result of the NAFTA, Canadian exports to Mexico will increase more than Mexican imports to Canada."[9]

Increased Mexican demand for Canadian exports will be fueled not only by the removal of Mexican trade barriers, but also by accelerated growth in Mexico resulting from its freer trade with the United States.

The Impact on Industrial Structure

Under free trade with the United States, Canada's exports have tended to grow less in its traditional industrial base and more in higher-value-added resource transformation, higher-technology industries, and services. Although its impact is expected to be much

---

8 A 1991 Bank of Montreal study found that Canada ranked ahead of Mexico in the following criteria contributing to locational advantage: availability and cost of capital; government regulations; labor-management relations; labor skills; macroeconomic and financial policies; marketing; political stability; product quality and design; productivity; quality of management; resource endowments; tax structure; technology; and transportation infrastructure. Cited by Lorraine Eden and Maureen Appel Molot, "Comparative and Competitive Advantage in the North American Trade Bloc," *Canadian Business Economics* 1 (Fall 1992): 45–59.

9 Watson, *Economic Impact*, p. 22.

smaller than that of the FTA, the NAFTA is likely to reinforce this trend, partly because of the general tariff reductions slated under the agreement and partly because of its provisions with respect to specific industries. Key effects are likely to be as follows:

- As with the FTA, there will be losers from the reorganization of industrial activity, particularly in labor-intensive sectors. Apparel, footwear, textiles, food processing, and certain machinery and industrial products using standard technology (such as small electrical appliances) are all sectors that may face greater competition as a result of the NAFTA although, for many of them, much of the adjustment and/or downsizing resulting from increased competition has already taken place under the FTA.

- Canadian and US firms will gain an advantage over firms in non-NAFTA countries in accessing large Mexican public sector procurement contracts — including those of the state-owned oil company, PEMEX — just at a time when the Mexican public sector is seeking to upgrade its infrastructure. This is important because Mexico is not currently a signatory to the procurement code of the General Agreement on Tariffs and Trade (GATT). Canadian firms in areas as diverse as oil and gas servicing and software are likely to find the government procurement provisions of the NAFTA very advantageous.

- The Mexican private sector is also expected to experience continued strong investment growth, supported by the key NAFTA protections afforded foreign investors. With supplementary NAFTA provisions toward the liberalization of such areas as travel for business persons, land transportation, telecommunications, and financial services, this trend promises benefits for exports of goods and services in several areas of Canadian expertise, such as telecommunications, banking, trucking, and environmental protection.

- Mexico's opening of its automotive sector is expected to have a positive impact on Canada, since most Mexican automotive imports were already entering Canada duty free, while Canadian exports were still virtually excluded from the Mexican market. Although Mexico is expected to continue increasing its share of the North American market for autos and parts, Canada's industry is much more likely to be able to hold its own by being fully integrated within the North American market than by excluding itself from a large part of it.

- The bulk of the NAFTA's agricultural provisions are expected to be favorable to Canadian producers because Canada's agriculture tends to complement that of Mexico. In particular, the NAFTA will encourage Mexico to import more cereals and meat products from both Canada and the United States.

Could Canada Have Avoided These Changes?

Could Canada have avoided the short-run adjustment costs in some of the import-competing sectors mentioned above by staying out of the NAFTA and thus forgoing the gains from liberalized trade — in particular, in its export sectors?

As noted earlier, this seems unlikely because Canada would have had to face a substantial part (though not all) of the increased competition from Mexico in any case, since Mexico would have become more competitive due to its free trade arrangement with the United States. Moreover, Canadian firms would also have had to face stronger competition from US firms that would have been getting duty-free inputs from Mexico that would not have been available to firms in Canada.

In short, had Canada stayed out of the NAFTA, it would have had to face less competition from Mexico, but more from the United States, than by going in. Thus, it is unlikely that Canada would have faced less competition and less painful short-run adjustment costs.

This suggests that opponents of the NAFTA — and even many of its supporters — while recognizing the short-run costs of participating in the NAFTA, may have underestimated the short-run costs of failing to participate. In fact, the standard assessment of the net effects of free trade — that is, the long-run benefits minus the short-run adjustment costs — is no longer appropriate for an existing member of a free trade area (in this case, Canada) when it is considering free trade participation with a new member (in this case, Mexico). Instead, the proper assessment for existing member Canada is the long-run benefits minus the greater adjustment costs from free trade participation — net of the disadvantages of nonparticipation — with new member Mexico.

These considerations suggest that, in general, no country facing Canada's decision is able to avoid adjustment costs. In Canada's case, this conclusion has been confirmed by a post-NAFTA development, the completion of the Uruguay Round of the GATT: had Canada not participated in the NAFTA, the successful GATT negotiations would have forced Canada to face many of its NAFTA adjustments in any case.

It is not possible for any country to escape the adjustments required in a world of changing trade conditions. In such a world, the status quo has ceased to be an option. The choice for any trading nation is not whether or not to adjust, but whether to put in place policies that will encourage adjustment or, more painfully, attempt to resist it.

Chapter 11

Constraints on Government Policy

Canada participates in a number of international agreements and organizations that, in combination, form a rules-based system of international relations. It is the purpose of these agreements to mutually constrain government behavior in certain areas, where such constraints are understood to enhance the common good of parties to the agreement. For example, Canada is currently prevented by the General Agreement on Tariffs and Trade (GATT) from increasing its tariffs against the products of low-wage countries; it is obligated under the International Energy Agreement to share its oil in the event of an international energy crisis; and it must contribute large sums of money every year toward the functioning of the United Nations as a cost of membership in that organization. Canada voluntarily agrees to abide by these rules and obligations because they tend, on the whole, to protect and promote the common good of the countries involved and — in the case of trade obligations, in particular — to prevent large economies from bullying smaller ones.

On balance, the NAFTA, like any other trade agreement, puts some constraints on the policies of all its signatories. Like many other trade agreements, however, it also exempts a number of sensitive sectors from its generally applicable obligations. What kinds of constraints does the NAFTA put on the policies of Canadian governments? What sectors or policies are exempt from these constraints? What could be the impact of these constraints and exemptions on the economic development or social policies of present or future Canadian governments? Would rejecting the NAFTA have freed Canadian governments from the constraints and ensured permanence for the exemptions? We will attempt to answer these questions in turn.

Types of Constraints
Created by the NAFTA

National Treatment

Except for the numerous sectors and policies that are exempt from the agreement's obligations altogether (see the last section of this chapter), the NAFTA in general requires that goods, services, or investors of one party to the agreement be given treatment no less favorable within the territory of another party than that which the latter party accords its own goods, services, or investors. In other words, a government in a NAFTA country is generally free to follow any policy it wishes, provided it applies that policy equally to firms and investors based in other NAFTA countries.

This "national treatment" principle of nondiscrimination is one of the basic principles of the GATT. National treatment *permits each country to apply its own laws, regulations, and other requirements according to its own objectives*, while at the same time fulfilling its trade obligations — and enjoying trade benefits in return — by not discriminating against its trading partners. Thus, as a constraint, national treatment is weaker and less damaging to sovereignty than is "harmonization," which obliges parties to follow the same policies, or "mutual recognition," which obliges countries to accept goods, services, or investments regulated by or made according to the product standards of another jurisdiction — as, for example, in the European Union. The principle of national treatment is key to understanding the functioning of the NAFTA, as it was with respect to the Canada-US Free Trade Agreement (FTA) (see Box 2).

With respect to the policies of a state or province, national treatment usually means according other member countries treatment no less favorable than that which is accorded residents of another state or province of the same country. That is, the NAFTA

Box 2:   *National Treatment in the NAFTA*

The principle of national treatment is underlined in the following NAFTA articles:

- Article 301 states that the parties grant each other's goods national treatment under the terms of the GATT. Annex 301.3 lists for each country a limited number of policies or goods that will be exempt, such as, in the case of Canada, provincial controls on the export of unprocessed fish and, in the case of Mexico, many types of used machinery during the first ten years of the agreement.
- Article 904 states that national treatment applies to standards-related measures — that is, a party must as a rule apply the same standards to products from other NAFTA countries that it applies to its own.
- Article 1003 states that, for contracts covered by the NAFTA's government procurement provisions, governments cannot accord goods or services suppliers of another NAFTA country treatment less favorable than that which it accords its other suppliers, including its own nationals.
- Article 1102 states that national treatment applies with respect to the establishment, acquisition, expansion, management, conduct, operation, and sale and other disposition of investments. (This provision is subject to numerous exceptions.)
- Article 1202 states that each party "shall accord to service providers of another Party treatment no less favourable than that it accords, in like circumstances, to its own service providers." (There are also numerous exceptions to this provison.)
- Article 1703 states that national treatment applies to the protection and enforcement of all intellectual property rights — except in the case of sound recordings, for which one country can apply to another the reciprocal of the treatment its nationals receive in it.

---

leaves current provincial policies untouched if they apply to nationals of other NAFTA countries in the same way that they apply to out-of-province Canadian firms or investors. With respect to standards-related measures, however, each of the federal governments must seek to ensure that provincial or state governments, as well as nongovernmental standardizing bodies, also observe the rights and obligations pertaining to nondiscriminatory treatment set out in the chapter on standards-related measures.

This being said, there are numerous exceptions under which Canadian governments at all levels will continue to be allowed to discriminate against all foreigners, including persons and businesses based in other NAFTA countries. Some of the more important ones are described below.

Policies Forbidden
Outright by the NAFTA

Few economic policies — and certainly no social policies — are forbidden outright by the NAFTA. The most important types of policies that are forbidden — in addition, of course, to trade restrictions at a border within the NAFTA — are certain performance requirements. Thus, a NAFTA government cannot refund or waive customs duties owed by a producer located on its territory, *if the refund is conditional*, for example, on that producer's reaching a certain export level or giving preference to locally produced goods. Similarly, a NAFTA signatory may not require that an investor on its territory — be it a domestic investor, one from another NAFTA country, or one from a non-NAFTA country — achieve a particular performance with respect, for example, to exports, domestic content, or net foreign exchange inflows.

In other words, policies that directly impose certain performance requirements that are potentially harmful to competitors in other NAFTA countries[1] — are judged inappropriate in a free trade area, where the aim is precisely to open up borders to competition. These interdictions apply equally to all parties, although Canada and Mexico retain the important right to refuse entry altogether to investments over a certain threshold, and Canada will continue to provide duty waivers (remissions) to auto pact producers.

---

1 For example, the requirement that a producer give preference to locally produced goods damages the competitive position of firms in other NAFTA countries.

Policies Mandated by the NAFTA

In addition, the NAFTA mandates that its member governments provide the following "minimum treatments" of firms and investors from other NAFTA countries:

* *Most-favored-nation treatment*: If a NAFTA government signs a trade agreement that gives a non-NAFTA country certain concessions — beyond those provided to its NAFTA partners — in a sector covered by the NAFTA obligations, that government is obligated to extend the same treatment to its NAFTA partners.

* *Openness in public sector procurement*: In procurement areas covered by the NAFTA, the deal mandates policies that ensure openness in the tendering process and fairness in the awarding of bids.

* *Protection of investors against arbitrary expropriation*: This provision does not alter the spirit of current Canadian policies toward domestic or foreign investors, since private businesses already have recourse to Canadian tribunals in the event that they claim to have been unfairly expropriated. Specific policies prohibited by the NAFTA include setting royalty payments at such levels that they effectively constitute expropriation.

* *Protection of intellectual property*: As North American economies increasingly become information based and knowledge intensive, protection against theft of intellectual property such as patents will be of ever greater benefit to Canadian researchers, writers, and artists, among others earning a living in creative fields. In return, Canada is committed to providing protection of intellectual property rights to individuals and businesses from other NAFTA countries.

Panel Review of Antidumping and Countervailing Duty Decisions

Determinations concerning antidumping and countervailing duties by the relevant administrative agencies — in Canada's case, the

Canadian International Trade Tribunal — are liable under the NAFTA to be reviewed by a trinational panel of experts, as they were under the FTA. Like other NAFTA obligations, this one applies equally to the three member countries. But because duties imposed by the large market — the United States — damage Canadian and Mexican exporters far more than Canadian and Mexican duties damage US exporters, the benefits of this provision, which deters the application of such duties, are likely to accrue most to Canada and Mexico.

Exemptions from NAFTA Rules

The NAFTA cannot be understood or judged without reference to the numerous exemptions that are clearly defined in its various chapters and, in particular, in the annexes to the agreement. These specifically remove entire areas — for example, for Canada, social services and cultural policies — from the reaches of the services and investment provisions of the agreement (see Chapter 5 of this book). Other notable exemptions from the NAFTA, in addition to Canada's protection of agricultural marketing boards, include certain types of federal procurement (for example, for research and development purposes); also, many provincial and municipal procurement practices will not even come under scrutiny under the terms of the deal. Finally, nothing in the agreement can prevent a signatory from taking any action it considers necessary for the protection of its essential security interests.

Except in some specified circumstances — for example, if a new tax amounts to discriminatory expropriation — the NAFTA does not apply to taxation measures, and international tax conventions to which a NAFTA country is a party will prevail over the NAFTA.

The Effect of the Constraints and Exemptions

In summary, the NAFTA's main constraints and exemptions are as follows:

- The agreement adopts the principle of national treatment, which does not require the harmonization of policies, but states that laws and standards must be applied equally to foreign and domestic investors.
- It forbids certain performance requirements.
- It adopts minimum standards, notably in the area of investor treatment, intellectual property, and due process.
- It spells out exceptions to national treatment that allow members to treat domestic and other NAFTA-based firms differently.

Among the misconceptions about the NAFTA is that it encroaches on Canada's ability to pursue a wide range of domestic policies. It is therefore worth noting that the NAFTA does not prevent the Canadian government from

- adopting any tax or social policy it chooses;
- subsidizing firms under certain circumstances — for example, in return for specific investment or research commitments — without having to worry about countervailing duties;
- extending research and development contracts to leading-edge Canadian firms;
- nationalizing industries or setting up public monopolies in any sector; or
- setting any standard it chooses, for example, to support sustainable development objectives.

On the face of it, these provisions are of huge benefit to Canada, which, as a smaller trading nation, benefits from the rule of law as opposed to the use of unilateral trade sanctions in the resolution of trade disputes.

Chapter 12

Conclusion

This study has sought to provide a guide to the NAFTA and to give Canada's participation in it a global and historical context. We have argued that, although deeper global economic integration does pose serious challenges to particular segments of the economy and the labor market in a rich industrial economy such as Canada's, it is practically impossible to sidestep those challenges by shrinking from global or regional trade agreements. By participating in the NAFTA, Canada gets a chance to shape the rules by which the integration of developed and developing economies will unfold, and can maximize the benefits it will derive from increased global trade.

In our view, Canada's entry into the NAFTA fits in with its long-run trade policy objectives. Although Canada has been a committed formal participant in successive rounds of negotiations under the General Agreement on Tariffs and Trade (GATT), the deepening of its bilateral relationship with the United States has been a historical fact, sustained by numerous trade agreements between the two countries over the years. Canada could hardly afford to ignore its major trading partner's Mexican initiative, and would have been right to oppose it if it had endangered multilateral free trade. This, we argued, was not the case, as the recent successful conclusion to the Uruguay Round of multilateral trade talks conclusively demonstrated. Indeed, many of the issues settled during the most recent round of those talks — for example, the inclusion of free trade in services, the treatment of trade-related investment measures, and the protection of intellectual property — were previewed in the NAFTA.

The NAFTA itself is a lengthy document that not only builds significantly on GATT rules and on the Canada-US Free Trade Agreement (FTA), but also contains some truly innovative features. In many areas, the NAFTA is more detailed and provides for more comprehensive rules than did either the GATT or the FTA.

In particular, the NAFTA improves on a number of existing technical measures pertaining to trade in goods — for example, customs rules — which will make it easier for exporters to benefit from the tariff reductions mandated by the agreement. The NAFTA significantly opens North American trade in many sectors — notably agriculture, textiles, automobiles, and computers — which will result in the greater integration of Mexico's economy with the economies of the other two partners. In many cases, it is Mexico that must undergo the most radical opening of its markets as a result of the NAFTA, since the Canadian and US markets were already relatively open to Mexican products.

The NAFTA also makes much progress in opening up Mexico's financial and telecommunications sectors, as well as laying the groundwork for the future liberalization of trade in all services among the three countries. It provides for freer travel for business purposes, increases protection for investors, and embodies the new GATT protections for intellectual property rights. The deal also makes significant progress in opening public sector procurement in Mexico to businesses located in the other two member countries, and expands on the procurement package between Canada and the United States that was contained in the bilateral FTA.

The NAFTA embodies each country's right to set the environmental, health, and safety standards it deems necessary, and to apply the necessary measures to enforce them, even if these result in reduced trade or investment among the three signatories. The parallel accords to the NAFTA also provide for the use of trade penalties should Mexico persistently fail to enforce its own environmental laws — something it has been guilty of in the past, according to many critics. Fears that the NAFTA may result in a "race to the bottom" by the three countries in terms of environmental and labor standards seem to us to lack solid grounds: there appears to be no historical evidence that free trade produces such results.

This being said, although certain sectors will see immediate tangible benefits from the opening of the Mexican market, the NAFTA is expected to provide only modest net economic benefits for Canada relative to the size of its economy, and, for some industries, it will result in an increased competitive challenge from both Mexico and the United States. But if Canada had chosen not to participate, it would have been excluded from most of the benefits of the NAFTA, and left vulnerable to virtually all of the agreement's costs. It would also have put the United States in the position of being a continental "hub," with Canadian and Mexican "spokes," an arrangement that would have reduced Canada's attractiveness as an investment location.

The deal's disappointments, from a Canadian perspective, are mainly in the nature of its failure to open up the North American market even more through less stringent rules of origin, a different approach to antidumping and countervailing duty disputes, and a general assurance of reciprocity of treatment for Canadian firms in the United States with respect, for example, to financial services. Although these problems are not new, resolving them would have helped make Canada a more attractive investment location within the free trade area.

In conclusion, it seems clear that Canada will be better off as a participant in the NAFTA than it would have been as an outsider to an emerging hemispheric free trade area. Had it rejected the agreement, Canada might have suffered substantial losses in both its competitive stature and its share of North American direct investment, and such losses, once incurred, would have been difficult to make up. The deal is not a panacea for Canada's trade problems. The realization of the full potential benefit of the NAFTA for Canadian business hinges on continuing progress toward the removal of the remaining barriers to trade in North America, for which a narrow avenue is now provided in the planned bilateral negotiations with the United States and Mexico on a new antidumping and subsidies regime.

Selected References

Anderson, Terry L., ed. *NAFTA and the Environment*. San Francisco: Pacific Research Institute for Public Policy, 1993.

Belous, Richard S., and Jonathan Lemco, eds. *NAFTA as a Model of Development: The Benefits and Costs of Merging High and Low Wage Areas*. Washington, DC: National Planning Association, 1993.

Berry, Al, Leonard Waverman, and Ann Weston. "Canada and the Enterprise for the Americas Initiative: A Case of Reluctant Regionalism." *Business Economics* 15 (April 1992).

Boddez, Thomas M., and Michael J. Trebilcock. *Unfinished Business: Reforming Trade Remedy Laws in North America*, Policy Study 17. Toronto: C.D. Howe Institute, 1993.

Canada. Department of Finance. *The North American Free Trade Agreement: An Economic Assessment from a Canadian Perspective*. Ottawa: Supply and Services Canada, 1992.

Canada. Royal Commission on the Economic Union and Development Prospects for Canada [Macdonald Commission]. *Report*, 3 v. Ottawa: Supply and Services Canada, 1985.

Chambers, Edward J., and Phillip Raworth. "Western Canada–Mexico Trade: Realizing Strategic Opportunities." *Western Canada Economic Diversity* (Canada West Foundation) (March 1993).

Economic Council of Canada. *Venturing Forth: An Assessment of the Canada-US Trade Agreement*. Ottawa: Supply and Services Canada, 1988.

Eden, Lorraine, and Maureen Appel Molot. "Comparative and Competitive Advantage in the North American Trade Bloc." *Canadian Business Economics* 1 (Fall 1992): 45–59.

————, and Maureen Appel Molot. *The NAFTA's Automotive Provisions: The Next Stage of Managed Trade*, C.D. Howe Institute Commentary 53. Toronto: C.D. Howe Institute, November 1993.

Faux, Jeff, and Richard Rothstein. *Fast Track, Fast Shuffle: The Economic Consequences of the Administration's Proposed Trade Agreement with Mexico*. Ottawa: Canadian Centre for Policy Alternatives, April 1991.

Gaston, Noel, and Daniel Trefler. "The Labour Market Consequences of the Canada-US Free Trade Agreement: A Preliminary Assessment." University of Toronto, October 1992. Mimeographed.

Gestrin, Michael, and Alan M. Rugman. *The NAFTA's Impact on the North American Investment Regime*, C.D. Howe Institute Commentary 42. Toronto: C.D. Howe Institute, March 1993.

Golt, Sidney. *The GATT Negotiations, 1986–90: Origins, Issues, and Prospects.* London; Washington, DC; Toronto: British-North American Committee, 1988.

Harris, Richard, and David Cox. *Trade, Industrial Policy, and Canadian Manufacturing*, Ontario Economic Council Research Study 31. Toronto: Ontario Economic Council, 1983.

International Monetary Fund. "Mexico: The Strategy to Achieve Growth," Occasional Paper 99. Washington, DC, September 1992.

Hufbauer, Gary Clyde, and Jeffrey J. Schott. *NAFTA: An Assessment.* Washington, DC: Institute for International Economics, 1993.

Johnson, Jon R. *What Is a North American Good? The NAFTA Rules of Origin*, C.D. Howe Institute Commentary 40. Toronto: C.D. Howe Institute, February 1993.

Josling, Tim, and Rick Barichello. *Agriculture in the NAFTA*, C.D. Howe Institute Commentary 43. Toronto: C.D. Howe Institute, April 1993.

Krajewski, Stephen. *Intrafirm Trade and the New North American Business Dynamic*, Conference Board of Canada Report 88-92. Ottawa: Conference Board of Canada, 1992.

Lipsey, Richard G. *Canada at the US-Mexico Free Trade Dance: Wallflower or Partner?* C.D. Howe Institute Commentary 20. Toronto: C.D. Howe Institute, August 1990.

———. *Notes on Globalisation and Technological Change and Canadian Trade Policy*, CIAR Program in Economic Growth and Policy, Working Paper 8. Toronto: Canadian Institute for Advanced Research, February 1993.

———, and Murray G. Smith. *Taking the Initiative: Canada's Trade Options in a Turbulent World*, Observation 27. Toronto: C.D. Howe Institute, 1985.

———, and Robert C. York. *Evaluating the Free Trade Deal: A Guided Tour through the Canada-US Agreement*, Policy Study 6. Toronto: C.D. Howe Institute, 1988.

Loizides, Stelios, and Gilles Rhéaume. "The North American Free Trade Agreement: Implications for Canada." Report 99-93. Ottawa: Conference Board of Canada, 1993.

Mace, Gordon, and Gérard Hervouet. "Canada's Third Option: A Complete Failure?" *Canadian Public Policy* 15 (December 1989): 387–404.

Nicholls, Christopher. *Government Procurement and Canada-US Trade*, Ontario Centre for International Business Working Paper WP 1992-49. Toronto: Ontario Centre for International Business, 1992.

Ontario. Treasurer of Ontario. *Renewing Ontario: A Plan for the Economy.* Toronto: Ministry of Treasury and Economics, 1992.

Organisation for Economic Co-operation and Development. "Survey of Mexico". Paris, December 1992.

Ostry, Sylvia. *Governments and Corporations in a Shrinking World.* New York: Council on Foreign Relations, 1990.

Pauly, Peter. "Macroeconomic Effects of the Canada-US Free Trade Agreement," Studies on the Economic Future of North America series. Vancouver; Toronto: Fraser Institute and University of Toronto Centre for International Studies, 1991.

Perry, J. Harvey. "The Great Trade Debate." *Tax Memo* (Canadian Tax Foundation) 71 (August 1986).

Plourde, André. *Energy and the NAFTA*, C.D. Howe Institute Commentary 46. Toronto: C.D. Howe Institute, May 1993.

Royal Bank of Canada. "Economic Restructuring in Canada." *EconoViews* (August 1993).

Sauvé, Pierre, and Brenda González-Hermosillo. *Implications of the NAFTA for Canadian Financial Institutions*, C.D. Howe Institute Commentary 44. Toronto: C.D. Howe Institute, April 1993.

Schwanen, Daniel. *A Growing Success: Canada's Trade Performance under Free Trade*, C.D. Howe Institute Commentary 52. Toronto: C.D. Howe Institute, September 1993.

Smith, Arthur J.R. "Canada's Policy Problems." In H.E. English, ed. *Canada and the New International Economy.* Toronto: University of Toronto Press, 1961.

Trebilcock, Michael J. "The Future of the World Trading Regime: Multilateralism or Regionalism? Free Trade or Fair Trade?" Ontario Centre for International Business Working Paper 1992-42. Toronto: University of Toronto, Faculty of Law, International Business and Trade Law Programme; York University, Osgoode Hall Law School, 1992.

Tremblay, Rodrigue. "L'Émergence d'un bloc économique et commercial nord-américain: la compétitivité de l'économie canadienne et la politique du taux de change." Université de Montréal, cahier 9212, 1992.

United States. Congress. Congressional Budget Office. *Agriculture in the North American Free Trade Agreement*. Washington, DC: Congressional Budget Office, May 1993.

Watson, William G. *The Economic Impact of the NAFTA*, C.D. Howe Institute Commentary 50. Toronto: C.D. Howe Institute, June 1993.

————. *Environmental and Labor Standards in the NAFTA*, C.D. Howe Institute Commentary 57. Toronto: C.D. Howe Institute, February 1994.

Waverman, Leonard. "The NAFTA Agreement: A Canadian Perspective." In Steven Globerman and Michael Walker, eds. *Assessing NAFTA: A Trinational Analysis*. Vancouver: Fraser Institute, 1993.

Wonnacott, Ronald J. "Canadian Trade Policy for the 1990s." *Policy Options* 14 (July-August 1993).

————. *The Economics of Overlapping Free Trade Areas and the Mexican Challenge*. Toronto; Washington, DC: Canadian-American Committee, 1991.

————. *The NAFTA: Fortress North America?* C.D. Howe Institute Commentary 54. Toronto: C.D. Howe Institute, October 1993.

————. *US Hub-and-Spoke Bilaterals and the Multilateral Trading System*, C.D. Howe Institute Commentary 21. Toronto: C.D. Howe Institute, October 1990.

————, and Paul Wonnacott. *Free Trade between the United States and Canada: The Potential Effects*. Cambridge, Mass.: Harvard University Press, 1967.

World Bank. *World Development Report, 1993*. Washington, DC, 1993.

Members of the
C.D. Howe Institute[*]

---

[*] The views expressed in this publication are those of the authors and do not necessarily reflect the opinions of the Institute's members.

E. Kendall Cork
William J. Cosgrove
Co-Steel Inc.
Pierre Côté
Cott Corporation
J.G. Crean
Crestbrook Forest Industries Ltd.
John Crispo
Devon Gaffney Cross
Crown Life Insurance Company Limited
Thomas P. d'Aquino
Leo de Bever
W. Ross DeGeer
Deloitte & Touche
Desjardins Ducharme Stein Monast
Robert Després
Deutsche Bank (Canada)
John H. Dickey
Iain St. C. Dobson
The Dominion of Canada General
    Insurance Company
Marcel Dutil
Gordon H. Eberts
The Empire Life Insurance Company
H.E. English
ENSIS Corporation
Ernst & Young
Export Development Corporation
Ronald J. Farano, Q.C.
Field & Field Perraton Masuch
First Marathon Securities Limited
Aaron M. Fish
John P. Fisher
Fishery Products International Limited
C.J. Michael Flavell, Q.C.
Fleck Manufacturing Inc.
Ford Motor Company of Canada, Limited
Formula Growth Limited
L. Yves Fortier, C.C., Q.C.
Four Seasons Hotels Limited
GSW Inc.
General Electric Canada Inc.
General Motors of Canada Limited
Gluskin Sheff + Associates Inc.
Goodman & Goodman
Peter Goring
The Great-West Life Assurance Company

Greyhound Lines of Canada
Morton Gross
Le Groupe Secor Inc.
Groupe Sobeco Inc.
H. Anthony Hampson
C.M. Harding Foundation
G.R. Heffernan
Lawrence L. Herman
Hewlett-Packard (Canada) Ltd.
Hill & Knowlton Canada
Home Oil Company Limited
Gordon J. Homer
Honeywell Limited
Hongkong Bank of Canada
The Horsham Corporation
Dezsö Horváth
Human Resources Association of
    Nova Scotia
H. Douglas Hunter
Hydro-Québec
IBM Canada Ltd.
Imasco Limited
Imperial Oil Limited
Inco Limited
Inland Cement Limited
The Insurance Bureau of Canada
Interprovincial Pipe Line Inc.
Investors Group Inc.
IPSCO Inc.
Tsutomu Iwasaki
The Jarislowsky Foundation
Robert Johnstone
KPMG Peat Marwick Thorne
Mark D. Kassirer
Joseph Kruger II
Lac Minerals Ltd.
R.William Lawson
Jacques A. Lefebvre
Gérard Limoges
London Life Insurance Company
J.W. (Wes) MacAleer
McCallum Hill Companies
McCarthy Tétrault
MacDonald, Dettwiler & Associates Ltd.
McKinsey & Company
Maclab Enterprises
James Maclaren Industries Inc.

Laurent Thibault
3M Canada Inc.
The Toronto Dominion Bank
Toronto Star Newspaper Limited
The Toronto Stock Exchange
TransAlta Utilities Corporation
TransCanada PipeLines Limited
Trimac Limited
Trizec Corporation Ltd.
Robert J. Turner
Unilever Canada Limited
Urgel Bourgie Limitée
Vancouver Stock Exchange
Gustavo Vega Cánovas

Manon Vennat
VIA Rail Canada Inc.
J.H. Warren
West Fraser Timber Co. Ltd.
Westcoast Energy Inc.
George Weston Limited
Weston Road Wholesale Lumber Ltd.
Alfred G. Wirth
M.K. Wong & Associates Ltd.
Wood Gundy Inc.
Fred R. Wright
Xerox Canada Inc.
Paul H. Ziff

Honorary Members

G. Arnold Hart
David Kirk
Paul H. Leman

A.M. Runciman
J. Ross Tolmie, Q.C.